That's the Way I Think

Dyslexia, dyspraxia and ADHD explained

Second edition

David Grant

With illustrations by
Hannah Evelyn French

Routledge
Taylor & Francis Group

LONDON AND NEW YORK

First edition published 2005
by David Fulton Publishers

This edition published 2010
by Routledge
2 Park Square, Milton Park, Abingdon, Oxon, OX14 4RN

Simultaneously published in the USA and Canada
by Routledge
270 Madison Avenue, New York, NY 10016

*Routledge is an imprint of the Taylor & Francis Group,
an informa business*

© 2007, 2010 David Grant

Typeset in Goudy by
Florence Production Ltd, Stoodleigh, Devon
Printed and bound in Great Britain by
TJ International Ltd, Padstow, Cornwall

British Library Cataloguing in Publication Data
A catalogue record for this book is available from the British Library

Library of Congress Cataloging-in-Publication Data
Grant, David.
    That's the way I think: dyslexia, dyspraxia and ADHD explained/
David Grant. – 2nd ed.
        p. cm.
    1. Dyslexia. 2. Apraxia. 3. Attention-deficit hyperactivity
disorder. I. Title.
    RC394.W6G73 2010
    616.85'53 – dc22   2009034219

ISBN10: 0–415–56465–4 (hbk)
ISBN10: 0–415–56464–6 (pbk)
ISBN10: 0–203–85796–8 (ebk)

ISBN13: 978–0–415–56465–6 (hbk)
ISBN13: 978–0–415–56464–9 (pbk)
ISBN13: 978–0–203–85796–0 (ebk)

That's the Way I Think

Many people with dyspraxia and dyslexia also have ADHD. This fully revised edition of David Grant's thought-provoking, insightful book develops our understanding of specific learning differences and considers the further challenges presented by these overlapping conditions.

New sections explore mental imagery (visualisation) and synaesthesia, enabling the reader to gain a fuller understanding of the sensory experiences and thoughts of individuals with specific learning differences.

As well as providing information defining dyslexia, dyspraxia and ADHD, *That's the Way I Think* addresses topics including:

- colours and reading
- becoming creative
- sports, genes and evolution
- 'invisible' girls and women.

The accessible style of this book, which includes numerous anecdotes and personal insights, will immediately strike a chord with anyone who has first- or second-hand experience of these specific learning differences.

Essential and enlightening reading for people with specific learning differences as well as their parents and/or partner, this book also provides an invaluable insight for teachers, teaching assistants and SENCos.

David Grant is a chartered psychologist specialising in the identification of specific learning differences in adults. He is a regular speaker at conferences, and has over thirty years' experience of working in higher education.

Contents

Preface

There is nothing unusual about being dyslexic, dyspraxic or an individual with ADHD. About one in 20 people are dyslexic. About one in 20 are dyspraxic. About one in twenty have ADHD. However, in spite of these numbers, relatively few books have been written for adult dyslexics and dyspraxics that explore and explain in everyday language their lived experiences.

This book provides a non-academic explanation of why the everyday experiences of dyslexics, dyspraxics and individuals with ADHD are different from those of other people in a number of crucial ways. It was written for more than just adults and those in their late teens with a specific learning difference. As so many have pointed out to me, they also want members of their own family and close friends to gain a better insight into why they do certain things, and why they think in different ways.

Many also pointed out to me that they want people they work with and work for, whether that be colleagues, employers, teachers or lecturers, to also understand them. All too frequently dyslexics, dyspraxics and individuals with ADHD are misunderstood, and have been for far too long. This book is about dispelling myths and breaking down barriers of misunderstanding. It is written for non-professionals and professionals who want a clear insight into understanding the everyday lived experiences of being dyslexic, or being dyspraxic, or being someone with ADHD. This understanding is the key to unleashing talent and hidden potential.

Foreword

How many times in my teaching career spanning twenty-five years did I come across a child who was struggling with spelling, writing, reading or numeracy? An individual who did not appear to be making the same progress as their classmates, or worse, was not making progress at all. My natural teaching instinct told me to change the way I was teaching, provide an alternative stimulus, differentiate the work I was giving the individual child – but most of all to try to discover what the underlying difference was between this one child and their peers. What was often very obvious was that each individual had abilities as well as weaknesses and again the instinct was to build on the strengths and the abilities whilst trying to support the weaknesses.

Often, I was able to make a difference, but in hindsight, especially in the early days of my career, it was probably only transitory – the bigger issue was not being addressed. I can't remember any children being labelled dyslexic, dyspraxic or as having ADHD. Instead, they were slow learners, poor readers, clumsy, lazy or naughty. There were probably many other adjectives that were used by teachers and pupils alike that would

have had very negative connotations and may have
caused severe distress to those young people
encountering these difficulties. On reflection many
of these children would today have been assessed and
been given the label of dyslexia, dyspraxia and/or
ADHD.

Would having that label have made any difference to
my teaching? Probably not, because what I lacked was
knowledge about these specific learning differences and
the underlying meanings and emotions that become
what David defines as 'a lifestyle'. Why did I lack the
knowledge? Mainly because the research, assessment and
prolific writing that we now have on specific learning
differences was not available, and as a primary teacher I
used my knowledge of child development, different
teaching and learning styles and trial and error to try to
ensure that each individual in my classroom would be
able to reach their full potential. Looking back, I now
know that not all of those individuals would have
reached their full potential because I was not addressing
their underlying needs. David's book would without a
doubt have helped me all those years ago to have a
much deeper understanding of the needs of individuals
with these differences.

The book is written in an informal manner that is
accessible to everyone. There is much material about
dyslexia, but it is very academic in its nature, both in
terms of its content and its use of terminology and as
such is very dyslexia-unfriendly.

This book is different, it is written in an accessible
style that makes it very easy to read. The case studies

and references to the many individuals that David has worked with give you a sense of déjà vu, because every teacher or parent will be able to recognise the scenarios played out within the book and be able to name a young person they have known who will have encountered a similar difficulty.

The book is written for a multitude of audiences. First, those who are dyslexic, dyspraxic or who have ADHD who can empathise with the case studies drawn upon by David. Second, the parents and siblings of those with specific learning differences who want to understand their different way of thinking and be able to support them in everyday situations. Finally, it is written for professionals working with those with specific learning differences to support them in being able to provide the necessary teaching and learning opportunities that will meet their needs.

David has not only asked lots of questions; he has attempted to bring answers together and draw inferences from all of the personal histories that he has collected. When I was reading the book I began to question my knowledge and tried to address some of those underlying conceptions or misconceptions that I may have built up over the years in education. I hope that this book will make you reflect on your practice in the same way.

We have read much in the media about dyslexia and related specific learning differences. Much of the reporting would lead you to believe that there is one strategy, one piece of technology, one drug, one 'cure'. This book illustrates that one size does not fit all and that each individual has very personal requirements which, with help, support and intervention, can be managed and equip them with life-skills that will lead to a happy and fulfilling future.

Lorraine Petersen OBE
CEO of NASEN

Acknowledgements

This book could not have been written without over 2,000 dyslexics, dyspraxics and individuals with ADHD sharing with me their thoughts and experiences. To everyone, a big 'thank you'. I am also grateful, and humbled, by the emails, letters and phone calls I have received from individuals and families who have, for the first time, achieved an understanding of themselves, or child or partner, when reading the first edition of *That's the Way I Think*.

My family has also made a major contribution. My wife, Cathy, has helped me make my writing more succinct, questioned me on sections she did not understand, and improved my grammar. It is a better written book because of her input. My sons have also played a part. My eldest son, Matthew, played a key role in helping me establish a database. As a genetics student he cast a critical eye over my earlier observations and tracked down key papers. He also carried out a survey into the sleeping patterns of undergraduates. My youngest son, Daniel, is dyslexic and was the Middlesex 800m county champion in his age group for three successive years. Hence my particular interest in the links between sporting ability and dyslexia. As a sports and exercise science undergraduate (now a postgraduate MSc student) he helped in the gathering of data on the incidence of visualisation in undergraduates. I am very grateful for their inputs.

Hannah Evelyn French, an illustrator, graduated from Kingston University in 2003. I have always been impressed by how well, even as an undergraduate, she captured a range of dyslexic experiences in her work. As a dyslexic herself she could immediately understand what I was looking for whenever I asked her for an illustration. I am very pleased that Hannah has provided a new illustration – on visualisation – to accompany her previous ones.

Thanks are due to Tanya Watkins, fashion designer, for permission to use an illustration taken from her undergraduate portfolio. Tanya graduated in fashion from Kingston University with a first-class degree. I am also delighted that this second edition includes two illustrations by Kerry, a Ravensbourne College animation student. Kerry (a pseudonym) graduated in the summer of 2009. She is dyspraxic, has ADHD and is a synaesthete.

I am also grateful for the feedback from many university and college staff who encouraged me in my belief that there is still much of importance to be said about dyslexia, dyspraxia and ADHD.

Introduction

Dyslexia is far more than just a label – it is a life style. As a label it is associated with many different meanings and emotions. For some people, being told they are dyslexic is a moment of liberation: 'I was so anxious you were going to tell me I was thick. Knowing I'm dyslexic is the best day of my life.' For others, being told they are dyslexic is a surprise: 'I thought dyslexia was all about writing letters backwards. I don't do that so I thought I couldn't be dyslexic.'

This book is about both liberation and surprises. It is about liberation in the sense that even many people who know they are dyslexic don't fully understand what being a dyslexic is. It sets out to help develop and deepen personal understanding. This book is also about surprises, for there are many myths and misconceptions about dyslexia, and these are explored.

Issues of dyspraxia and ADHD (Attention Deficit Hyperactivity Disorder) as well as dyslexia are also discussed. Although they may at first sight appear quite different conditions, they have many features in common, and their overlap is much more extensive than many people realise. In addition, it is quite common to find they co-exist. For example, the combination of ADHD and dyspraxia is quite a frequent one.

This book is also about the individuality of people who are dyslexic, dyspraxic or have ADHD. The labels dyslexia, dyspraxia and ADHD are misleading for they suggest that everyone who is dyslexic, dyspraxic or has ADHD is exactly the same as another individual with the same specific learning difference. I prefer the terms 'dyslexias' and 'dyspraxias' because they help to break away from this misleading stereotyping. It is also useful to realise that ADHD can and does take different forms.

I also propose that being dyslexic or dyspraxic or an individual with ADHD should be considered as a life style – dyslexia is not just about difficulties with reading and spelling, dyspraxia is not just about clumsiness or difficulties with pronunciation, ADHD is not just about attentional difficulties. The presence of a specific learning difference means that your everyday life is influenced and shaped in a variety of different ways. This book explores those everyday experiences.

This book is purposely written in an informal style. The reason for this is simple – I have read too many books about dyslexia which are dyslexia-unfriendly because they are too academic. I wanted to write something that most dyslexic, dyspraxic and ADHD students would feel reasonably comfortable with. Second, many of the individuals I have met find it difficult to explain to others what being dyslexic, dyspraxic or an individual with ADHD is like since they are themselves unsure which of their experiences are due to their different way of thinking and which are not. I therefore wanted to write a book that their parents, partners and siblings could also read and learn from. I have chosen to illustrate the ideas and concepts by using the actual words of dyslexics, dyspraxics and individuals with ADHD I have met, for it is they who are living the experience.

In order to learn you have to listen. Many years ago Ewan McColl, a great songwriter, explained how he learnt from listening. He pointed out that when people are first asked questions about their lives, they spend the first twenty minutes telling you what they think you want to know. After that they tell you about themselves. By listening, it became very evident to me that being dyslexic or being dyspraxic or being an individual with ADHD is a lived experience that influences so many aspects of everyday life.

Over the past nine years I have listened to approximately 2,000 individuals with specific learning differences discussing their personal histories and everyday experiences. Mainly students in higher education, they ranged in age from 16 to 68. In spite of this collective wealth of experience, and very impressive levels of intellectual ability, the thing that struck me most was how little is still known and understood about dyslexia, dyspraxia or ADHD.

When you ask questions about dyslexia most people immediately think of some kind of difficulties with reading. It is not obvious that going into a room to collect something, only to find you have forgotten what you went for, might also be related to being dyslexic. It is even less obvious that using the time before drifting off to sleep to sort through the day's events and plan for the following day is also a frequent experience of individuals with dyslexia, as well as dyspraxia and ADHD. By creating space to listen, so much can be learnt.

Through listening carefully to detailed personal histories, I have gradually developed a much wider range of questions to draw upon when assessing whether a specific learning difference is present. This has taken me into unexplored areas. For example, the first edition of this book contained nothing on mental imagery. Since then I have realised just how important this sensory experience is and now routinely determine whether visualisation (including synaesthesia) is present, and if so, to what extent, when carrying out a diagnostic assessment. In that respect I am going back to the nineteenth-century tradition of psychology being the study of the mind.

I have also realised just how little I knew about ADHD when writing the first edition. As it was not until the autumn of 2008 that the National Institute for Clinical Excellence (NICE) advised the UK government that ADHD was a valid diagnosis, and that adults as well as children could have ADHD, I was not alone in my lack of understanding. However, I have since addressed this lack of knowledge and now routinely look for ADHD whenever I carry out an assessment. While I still have a great deal to learn, my diagnostic questioning has already revealed an intriguing association between ADHD and synaesthesia, an association explored in this new edition.

However, it is one thing to ask questions, but another matter to bring the answers together and draw inferences. The definition of a scientist as being someone who sees the same things as others but thinks about them differently is one that appeals to me. In one sense, virtually all the observations I have made could have been made 50 years ago. However, it does help to have an electronic database. The thinking differently is another matter. In writing this book I wanted to move beyond pure descriptions to also come up with possible explanations. This, at times, inevitably requires speculative thinking. Unlike most psychologists who study and research dyslexia, dyspraxia or ADHD, I had the advantage of not being wedded to one specific theory or hypothesis about underlying causes.

I could stand back. I also know from having taught about creativity and innovation for some years that new ideas often emerge from finding solutions to questions outside of the immediate field being studied. Standing back provides that space to think outside of the box. Consequently, the research literature I have consulted is unusually wide – taking in genetics, synaesthesia, the life histories of creative achievers, and cognitive neuropsychology.

Most of this research is published in academic journals and is written in a very complex and dense style, as it is aimed at researchers rather than the lay public. While I have drawn upon this research to inform my ideas and observations, I have avoided citing endless names and dates when writing each chapter. As it was my intention to keep the style of writing as informal as possible I have not included copious citations. My thinking has been informed by many different researchers and writers, but I would like to think it has also been inspired and shaped by the agent provocateur spirit of such great psychologists as Norman Geschwind.

Thinking outside of the box is an exciting adventure. You may not always be right but sometimes you can point ideas in a different direction. I sense that most research into dyslexia and dyspraxia, unlike a number of books I have read about ADHD, has somehow missed the person who is experiencing it. This second edition, like the first one, for me, is an attempt to get back to the person. I hope it is for you as well.

Chapter 1

Dyslexia, dyspraxia and ADHD

The common ground

Most books about dyslexia start by focusing on reading and spelling. Most books about dyspraxia begin by discussing problems with coordination. Most books about ADHD (Attention Deficit Hyperactivity Disorder) commence with an account of problems with concentration. These are important issues. They are not, however, the only issues. There are more common links between dyslexia and dyspraxia than distinguishing features. There are also many shared features with ADHD. That is why this book breaks with tradition by initially describing and discussing similarities rather than differences. This chapter focuses on those shared experiences – the common ground as it were. For many dyslexics, dyspraxics and individuals with ADHD, it is these experiences that most colour and shape their everyday lives. They are also often the most noticeable features.

Many of the students I see tell me how disorganised they are. In addition, they very often describe themselves as having a poor memory and poor concentration. Consequently they are likely to misplace things, forget what they were going to say halfway through a sentence, miss appointments, and make use of post-it notes and lists. They are also easily distracted, and experience difficulties when copying notes from an overhead projector as they find it hard to remember more than three or four words at a time.

All of these experiences, as well as many others, are the result of a weak working memory. This statement needs to be explained, for there are different types of memory, two of which are short-term memories: working memory and visuospatial memory. I am using the term 'working memory' to refer very specifically to a short-term memory for verbal information. For example, imagine you are new to a college or university and you ask someone how to get to the students union from where you are. When you are told, 'Go straight to the end of the corridor, turn left, and it's the third door on the right', you have to use your working memory to retain this information while you walk towards the students union. (If you can then retain a visual memory of this route once you have walked it then this is an example of a long-term visual memory.)

Working memory refers to a memory store that enables you to actively organise and think about verbal information for a short time. The term working memory is a better one than short-term memory for it captures the manner in which we think consciously about things. A key feature about working memory is that it is of limited capacity. Some people have a greater capacity than others.

In general, working memory capacity is linked to level of verbal reasoning. A high verbal reasoning ability is accompanied by an above-average working memory capacity. A low level of verbal reasoning ability is usually accompanied by a smaller working memory capacity. This harmony of linkage is not observed in most instances of dyslexia, dyspraxia or ADHD. As a fairly broad generalisation, the working memory space that is available for many individuals with a specific learning difference is less than they need for their level of ability. In many cases it is much less. In addition, working memory also appears to be more fragile, especially when ADHD is present.

The impact of limited working memory capacity

A lack of working memory capacity affects both academic life and everyday social and working life. For example, to take good notes in a lecture requires doing a number of different things at the same time. First, you need to be able to follow the theme of the lecture in order to understand the points that are being made. Second, you have to be able to identify what is important so you can make a note of the main points. That is, you have to know how to be selective. Third, you also need to be able to write down what is important. All these activities require the use of working memory space. On top of all this you have to be able to write quickly, spell well and maintain concentration.

Taking good notes can be difficult even for someone who does not have a specific learning difference. For a dyslexic, dyspraxic or individual with ADHD, note-taking is even more difficult because working memory space becomes overwhelmed very quickly, so some elements get squeezed out. As a consequence, doing more than one thing at a time becomes almost impossible when working memory is weak. For example, in a lecture some students just listen to make sure they have understood what is being said. Others try to take notes without really understanding what is being said. This is why being allowed to make a recording of a lecture is so important. It is also very helpful if a lecturer provides good-quality lecture notes, preferably in advance. A weak working memory also affects the copying of information. Most lecturers make use of either a PowerPoint presentation or an overhead projector. Poor reading skills obviously slow down the rate at which information can be read. However, a weak working memory also slows down the rate at which information can be copied.

If you have an efficient working memory, you can probably read through the following sentence and remember all of it while you write it down: 'Sperry was awarded the Nobel prize for his pioneering work in the 1930s on neuronal regeneration.' Being dyslexic, dyspraxic or an individual with ADHD will probably result in you remembering only a small part of the sentence while you are writing it down. Consequently, you have to spend more time looking from the text to your notes and back again when copying information down. You also have to scan to find your place again each time you go back to the text. Copying information down therefore takes considerably longer. If you also have to stop and think, 'How do I spell *pioneering*? How do I spell *neuronal*?' it can feel as if it is taking for ever to copy the information. While you are concentrating on remembering what it is you have to copy, there is no spare capacity to take in what the lecturer is saying. If you are an individual with ADHD even the act of maintaining concentration may well feel almost impossible.

Hannah's illustration (see Illustration 1.1) captures her own experience of being in a lecture. It is as if she is being so swamped by the words of the lecturer that she is no longer able to take in what is being said.

It is not surprising that most children and teenagers with specific learning differences find so many school lessons so frustrating. If a teacher starts off the lesson by saying, 'I want you do this, and then this, and when you have finished these make a start on this page of this exercise', by the time the teacher has reached the end of the list of things to do you will have forgotten what the first task was. You might then ask your friend what you have to do and this may be misinterpreted by the teacher as you not paying attention or being disruptive. In one or two subjects, such as maths, the difficulty with remembering more than a few things at a time makes it particularly hard to remember all the steps of a sequence that is being worked through.

A weak working memory does not necessarily mean you will be poor at maths. I have seen some brilliant mathematicians and physicists who have dyslexia, dyspraxia or ADHD. One captured the impact of his

Illustration 1.1

weak working memory quite succinctly: 'I find the easy maths difficult, and the difficult maths easy.' By easy maths he was referring to learning the times tables and doing mental arithmetic. By difficult maths he was referring to concepts such as matrices and calculus. Because a weak working memory often results in very noticeable difficulties with the learning of basic arithmetical processes such as multiplication and division, there is a danger that these difficulties will result in the suggestion that dyscalculia (a specific difficulty with numbers) is present. In my experience dyscalculia, which in its pure form is a fundamental difficulty with the concepts of 'greater than' and 'less than', is very rare.

A weak working memory also affects the writing of essays. Many students tell me that they find starting to write an essay 'the worse part'. This is not surprising. Writing an essay or report is like creating a complex story with lots of characters. As the writer, you have to decide what the story line is and the order of appearance of the characters. To plan and tell the story well requires lots of working memory capacity.

Limited working memory capacity makes it impossible to think about all aspects of the story at once because it imposes a limit on the number of ideas that can be actively considered at the same time. This results in the realisation that 'it's not going to work' and another attempt is made to think of how to organise all the ideas. And then another, and another, until frustration sets in and you go off to make a cup of tea or coffee instead. One student spoke for many when he referred to his difficulties with starting an essay as being 'the white sheet syndrome'. For many students, trying to work out how to start writing an essay is akin to looking at their ideas through a kaleidoscope. Each time they think about what to do the picture changes. The problem is that a limited working memory means that only part of the picture can be thought of at any one time, rather than the whole picture. It is therefore not surprising that the writing of an essay gets repeatedly put off until the last possible minute, even when an individual has started the preliminary research long before others.

Fortunately, there are ways of getting around these memory limitations. For a number of students with a specific learning difference, but not all, visual memory is much better than working memory. This means that mind-maps and spider-diagrams can be very useful. If these are drawn by hand they can get quite messy and this is why a software program such as Inspiration can be so important. (See Appendix for details of where to purchase specialist software.) By being able to drag ideas around on the screen and change text, the visual scheme of ideas can be kept very clean. The use of colour-coding and icons also makes it possible to group ideas together so links can be seen easily.

The difficulty with arranging ideas to arrive at an essay that has a good internal logic and structure means that many dyslexics and dyspraxics often have to rewrite an essay a number of times. It is not uncommon to be told, 'it takes me three times as long as anyone else'. Even making notes from books at the research stage for an essay can be problematic. Making notes requires an ability to select what is important. This involves being able to think about a number of ideas simultaneously so that only the most appropriate elements are selected.

A weak working memory also affects the structuring of sentences. Many dyslexics and dyspraxics have a tendency to write very long sentences that ramble. When memory is limited the whole of that working space might be taken up with just one phase, which then sparks the next idea, and then the next, and so on. Consequently, punctuation and internal logic suffer. Also, the completed 'sentence' will contain too many ideas, and will often go off at a tangent. Sometimes, the writing of a sentence will come to a complete halt due to stopping to think about a spelling. Because sorting this out can occupy all of the working memory capacity, it results in the original idea that was in the process of being written down being forgotten. Students tell me that when this happens they have to reread what they have just written in order to work out what they were going to say next. It is not surprising that so many students say they find it very hard to express their ideas in writing: 'I know it in my head but I can't get it down on paper'.

A weak working memory doesn't just have an impact on taking notes and writing essays, it affects everyday life as well. A high proportion of dyslexic, dyspraxic and ADHD students describe themselves as being disorganised, a 'bit dippy'. They give as examples forgetting appointments, misplacing and losing items, not returning books on time, and going to a room to fetch something only to find they have forgotten what they went for. Because forgetfulness is such a general problem, different people develop different coping strategies.

Some people have everything strewn around their room. Although this may appear to be disorganised, sometimes – and I stress the 'sometimes' – it can be a deliberate way of arranging things because everything is on display and visual memory can be used to remember where particular items are. Some students use their mobile phones as personal organisers and also text themselves messages of things they need to remember. Others use post-it notes and diaries. It is not unusual for someone with a weak working memory to write themselves a note on the back of their hand. Some students pack everything they need for the next morning the night before, to ensure things don't get forgotten when they leave the house the following morning. Others develop a routine of patting themselves, 'Have I got my wallet/watch/mobile/keys?', before going out of the house or leaving a pub.

A weak working memory is, in my experience, observed in most students with a specific learning difference. However, in a minority, more so in instances of dyspraxia and ADHD than dyslexia, working memory capacity is fine. As always, it is misleading to take a broad generalisation and apply it in all cases.

The fragility of working memory

Many students have told me how, during a conversation, ideas often occur to them suddenly and they go off at a tangent. On other occasions, they will be about to say something, only to realise they have forgotten what they wanted to say. Most students tell me how easily they can lose concentration, 'My mind wanders very easily', and how they were told off at school for daydreaming. These are all examples of the fragility of working memory. In one sense working memory has to be fragile in that new information is constantly replacing current information. However, the manner in which information is replaced appears to be much more of a random process for those with dyslexia, dyspraxia or ADHD than for individuals with no specific learning difference. I suspect that two factors may be responsible for this fragility: limited memory capacity and an inefficient executive function.

Limited memory capacity implies an imbalance between working memory capacity and verbal reasoning abilities. When a full psychological assessment is carried out using what is commonly known as the WAIS (Wechsler Adult Intelligent Scales) or WISC (Wechsler Intelligence Scales for Children), both working memory and verbal reasoning are measured. Ideally, these abilities should be in equilibrium. If, however, working memory capacity is much lower than the level required to be in balance with verbal reasoning, then a working memory deficit is formally recorded. It is important to note that working memory capacity does not have to be below average for a weak working memory to be recorded. I have seen a number of bright students who have scored higher on working memory than the average person. However, for these students there is still a significant gap between their scores for working memory and verbal reasoning.

When this imbalance occurs it is as if the brain is generating more ideas than can be accommodated within the available working memory space. This results in a logjam of ideas building up outside of working memory. Consequently, it is as if these ideas jostle competitively to gain access to the working memory space. Access to working memory is controlled by what psychologists call the executive function. This does a number of things, such as prioritising what information gains entry to working memory space, and controlling the direction of attention. Without such a mechanism our conscious experience of working memory would be one of total chaos. It also coordinates and integrates auditory and visual/spatial memories.

An analogy to illustrate this is to think of the executive function as being a bouncer outside a select nightclub – the more limited the working memory, the more select the nightclub. There is therefore great competition to gain entrance to this nightclub. When the nightclub is full the only way someone can gain entry is when someone else leaves. The greater the crowd outside, the more difficulties the bouncer will have, and the more chance there is of someone gatecrashing and getting past the bouncer without permission.

In the case of someone with a weak working memory the executive function is not particularly effective, with the consequence that ideas occur suddenly without warning. As they burst into working memory they create space by pushing an existing idea out of conscious thought. One student described this experience as feeling as if her ideas were being 'pushed over the edge'. Because ideas can come and go without warning the conscious thought experience of many individuals with dyslexia, dyspraxia or ADHD is characterised by a sense of chaos and transience of ideas (see Illustration 1.2).

This experience was summed up well by one dyslexic student of radio broadcasting. He described to me how, one evening in the student union bar, an idea suddenly occurred to him, an idea he thought was brilliant. 'Quick,' he said to his friend, 'write this idea down and phone me in the morning to tell me what it is.' He was well aware that if he didn't capture his creative idea

Illustration 1.2

there and then he would very quickly forget what it was. Sometimes thoughts can appear and disappear so rapidly they are like shooting stars, flashing across the conscious space of the mind. No sooner has an idea occurred than it vanishes.

I sometimes describe this experience, of ideas coming out of nowhere and then disappearing just as quickly, as being a kind of 'Richard Branson phenomenon'. Richard Branson is dyslexic and his Virgin company is very different from other commercial organisations. Most companies have a core business, such as making a specific kind of product, or selling a specific service. In contrast, the Virgin organisation is essentially a brand name, a very well known one that encompasses a diversity of activities, from music to financial services to drinks and travel. It is as if random ideas crash into Richard Branson's mind and grab his attention. He is, of course, skilled enough to discard ideas that won't work.

This fragility of thought appears to apply mainly to verbal thought. Visual thought seems to be more stable. For example, many dyslexic and dyspraxic students find they are very easily distracted when engaged in activities such as reading or writing. Although it could be argued that this is because they are not very interested in these activities, the same distractibility and unpredictability can also occur in conversation as well. One student told me: 'When an idea pops into my mind I have to say it straight away otherwise I will forget it.' Many students describe going off at tangents during a conversation. However, if engaged in a visual activity such as video editing, painting or drawing, or one with a high visual content such as playing hockey, football or sailing, then concentration can be intense and sustained, often for hours at a time. A key reason for this is that visual memory and thought take over and, in most cases, the visual memory capacity is considerably greater, particularly for dyslexics and individuals with ADHD. An exception to this is dyspraxia, for in about 50 per cent short-term visual memory is noticeably below expectation.

Many students have told me they have a very good memory for faces but are very poor at remembering names. Several art students have described how they try to overcome their poor memory for names by making sketches of the other students in their year and then writing the name of each student alongside the relevant sketch. Most people, whether dyslexic or not, are better at remembering faces than names. It is just that when working memory is poor the difficulty with remembering names becomes much more obvious.

Whilst the imbalance between a high level of verbal ability and a low working memory capacity results in memory retention being more fragile than it should be, in my experience ADHD dramatically speeds up the rate at which ideas enter and leave both verbal and visual conscious thought. When an idea enters working memory, it is as if it needs a small piece of Velcro to enable it to be held in conscious thought for a short time. In the case of ADHD, whenever an idea occurs it is as if the executive function coats it in soap instead of Velcro, making it slippery rather than sticky. Consequently, individuals with ADHD find it very hard to hold ideas in conscious thought, as they slide in and slip out rapidly and with an element of randomness. This slipperiness factor means that even when working memory capacity is good, forgetfulness is still very much an everyday experience and gives rise to what one student described as his 'disorganised mind'.

Processing speed

At the beginning of this chapter it was mentioned that a common link between dyslexia, dyspraxia and ADHD is a weak working memory. A second aspect they have in common is a slow speed of processing. Once again, this does not apply in all cases. However, it occurs with sufficient frequency to be recognised as an important feature.

In carrying out a psychological assessment using the WAIS, four general sets of abilities are assessed and their levels calculated. Two of these have already been mentioned – Working Memory and Verbal Reasoning (usually called Verbal Comprehension). The other two sets of abilities are Processing Speed and Perceptual Organisation (visual reasoning). Processing Speed is assessed by how well an individual does on two tasks, both of which are visual in nature and require an ability to take in and search for simple visual symbols very quickly. Although these two tasks involve a lower level of thinking than the three visual reasoning tasks that are used to determine a Perceptual Organisation score, they are important because they provide an indication of the speed at which simple or routine visual information can be processed and learnt without errors being made.

Ideally, the levels of Processing Speed and Perceptual Organisation should be in balance. For many dyslexics, dyspraxics and individuals with ADHD this is not the case: Processing Speed is often well below the level recorded for Perceptual Organisation. This difference will affect a wide range of activities, including speed of reading, writing and drawing, ability to proof-read well, and the types of sports and computer games that are preferred. Figure 1.1 for Alice, who is dyspraxic, is typical of the spiky WAIS profile recorded for many dyslexic, dyspraxic and ADHD individuals.

This characteristic profile reveals very clearly that scores for verbal and visual reasoning are much higher than scores for working memory and processing speed. (Note. If there was no specific learning difference, such as dyslexia, dyspraxia or ADHD, the WAIS profile would look fairly flat. That is, all four columns would be approximately the same height.) This characteristic double-spike profile occurs independently of age.

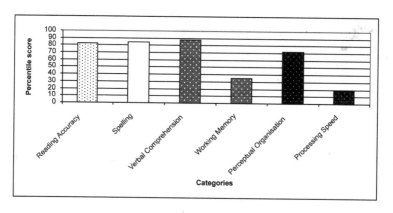

Figure 1.1 Alice's Reading and Spelling scores, plus 4 WAIS-III Index scores expressed as percentile scores

When dyslexia, dyspraxia or ADHD is present it does not matter whether someone is 8, 18 or 68 – the same profile is observed in about 80 per cent of instances of dyslexia, and probably about 60 to 70 per cent when dyspraxia or ADHD is present. You do not grow out of being dyslexic or dyspraxic even when special teaching improves reading skills or physiotherapy results in an improvement in motor coordination.

One way of interpreting this spiky profile is to think of the brain as a computer. Verbal Comprehension is akin to being the word processing software, whilst Working Memory is RAM memory. Perceptual Organisation can be thought of as the graphics card, and Processing Speed is the processing chip. For many dyslexics and dyspraxics, it is as if they have a good-quality word processing package and graphics card, but limited memory and a slow processing chip. However, it is not possible to go to the nearest computing store and buy additional memory and a faster chip. Instead, it is a question of learning how to get around the limitations so that full potential is achieved.

When processing speed is slow a number of activities are affected. For example, many students have told me that when they are writing they often feel as if their brain is thinking faster than their hand can move. Because of this, it is as if, at times, their hand jumps to keep up so parts of words or even whole words may be left out. When proof-reading, it is, as one student put it, 'As if my brain is ten words ahead of my eyes.' This is one key reason why proof-reading is so difficult. In fact, it can be so challenging that a number of students give up on it.

TextHELP is a software package that can read aloud text displayed on a computer screen. This can be a great help in proof-reading for you can listen to what you have written and check that it sounds right. Dragon Naturally Speaking is a software package that converts speech to text, taking away the slowness of writing by hand and difficulties with spelling. The software can learn to recognise most voices – but not all – within ten minutes (although it takes the user much longer to learn the commands).

A slow speed of processing will also affect reading. Reading requires doing many things simultaneously – you have to scan lines of visual symbols and discriminate very quickly between shapes, be able to understand what you are reading, as well as remember what you have just read. Whereas many dyslexics and dyspraxics are good at the verbal thinking requirements, if the processing is slow and working memory weak, the ability to understand and think about what has just been read will be disrupted. When there is an imbalance between speed of processing and speed of thought, it is not surprising that words get misread. It is as if part of the brain wants to go faster than it is receiving information, and it starts to make guesses at what a word might be.

A slow speed of processing also affects activities that require fast responses, such as some sports and computer games. One student who had reached the semi-professional level in football was puzzled why, even though he practised each day for hours at a time, he was always a fraction of a second off the pace. However, because of his excellent visual reasoning abilities, he could 'read' a game very well and was particularly good at defending. Once he had viewed his profile he immediately understood his strengths and weaknesses. Very few people reach a semi-professional level in sports. Many more people play computer games. In many cases, people with a much higher visual reasoning ability than processing speed prefer to play games of strategy rather than ones that depend purely on speed of response. This slowness of response can also be seen when scrolling through text on a computer monitor. If speed of processing is slow, rapid scrolling is very difficult even why reading skills are good.

Even activities such as crossing a busy road on foot, driving in traffic, or walking along a crowded pavement, can become slightly more difficult if processing speed is slow. When a slow processing speed is also accompanied by a weak short-term visual memory (this combination occurs in 50 per cent of dyspraxics), these types of everyday activities become even more challenging. A slow processing speed may also influence styles of drawing. This particular aspect is discussed in Chapter 7.

A slow speed of processing, in combination with a weak working memory, results in many dyslexics and dyspraxics disliking being asked to work under pressure. A number of students have told me that, provided they are left to work by themselves, they can achieve a high standard. But this has to be without pressure. Paradoxically, individuals with ADHD often work best under pressure. This, however, is a reflection of stress resulting in an increase in the production of those chemicals needed to improve the efficiency of how neurons in the brain 'talk' to each other.

To summarise what has been covered so far, a weak working memory and a slow speed of processing are typical aspects of being dyslexic, dyspraxic or an individual with ADHD. They are not, however, causes of any of these specific learning differences. Each factor influences a surprisingly wide variety of everyday experiences at home, work and college or university. Because of this it is appropriate to think of being dyslexic, dyspraxic or having ADHD as a particular kind of life style.

The next three chapters focus on the need to think about the different forms that the dyslexias, dyspraxias and ADHD can take.

Chapter 2

What is dyslexia?

Most definitions of dyslexia are too narrow for they focus on unexpected difficulties with learning to read. In reality dyslexia is extremely complex. This chapter begins with the simplistic view and goes on to describe and discuss the complexity that the dyslexias are.

Central to most definitions of dyslexia is the requirement that reading ability is unexpectedly poor, and that there is no adequate explanation to account for this other than dyslexia. As will be explained later, this is a narrow view of what dyslexia in reality is. However, in practice, this requirement has to be satisfied to arrive at a diagnosis of dyslexia, and this is the starting point for considering its complexity.

The only satisfactory way to determine whether reading skills are unexpectedly poor is to measure and compare an individual's level of intellectual ability with their level of reading performance. (Spelling ability is usually assessed at the same time as well.) A personal history is also required for if a difference is recorded the personal history will then help determine whether the difference is genuinely an unexpected one.

The question of which intellectual abilities to measure is crucial, since not all measures are suitable. In my view it is important to compare like with like. For this reason I place the greatest importance on the comparison of reading (and spelling) skills with verbal reasoning skills. Most diagnostic tests of verbal reasoning ability are carried out orally and measure knowledge and understanding of language through asking questions about the meaning of words and relationships between words.

Questions about the meanings of words typically take the form of 'Can you explain the meaning of the word "adolescent"?' Relationships between words are explored by asking questions such as 'In what ways are "drizzle" and "monsoon" similar to each other?' These questions are explored orally so that there are no reading or writing requirements. The questions are presented in sequence, going from quite simple questions to very hard ones. For example, most people can explain what a 'mountain' is. It is much harder to explain the meaning of the word 'paradigm'. As you would expect, some people are better at these kinds of tasks than others, but that is not important. What is important is how the score for an individual compares with that person's own scores for reading and spelling.

In general, the relationship between measures of verbal reasoning and reading and spelling abilities is an approximate one. That is, while there is a strong tendency for them to be roughly equal, some variation is to be expected. Nevertheless, for some people, the extent of the variation can be surprisingly great.

Jane is typical of many dyslexic students I see (see Figure 2.1). While her verbal reasoning performance places her in the top 20 per cent of the population, her word reading accuracy score puts her in the bottom 10 per cent. This is an unexpected difference given Jane's much higher level of verbal reasoning. If dyslexia were not present, her skills of reading and spelling would be at least average, and probably above.

There will probably always be debate about how big the gap has to be between levels of reading skills and verbal comprehension before dyslexia can be said to be present, but virtually all diagnoses of dyslexia are dependent on demonstrating an unexpected difference. Usually, if reading skills are weak, spelling is also weak. However, some people have very good reading skills but are very weak at spelling. Although it is a term not often used in the UK, the word 'dysorthographia' describes a person who has an unexpected weakness purely in spelling.

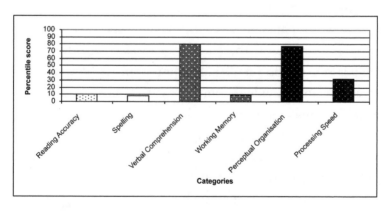

Figure 2.1 Jane's Reading and Spelling scores, plus 4 WAIS-III Index scores expressed as percentile scores

In order to demonstrate that a discrepancy between reading (and spelling) and verbal reasoning is an unexpected one, it is necessary to know key details about a person's life. For example one student, Shona, had been brought up in a country where even primary school children had to pay to be educated. Her family was very poor and her primary and secondary education totalled just eighteen months. Not unexpectedly, her skills of reading and spelling were below average, but by only a little. Shona's verbal reasoning skills were a little above average. Given the circumstances, her skills of reading and spelling were very much better than might have been expected. Shona was not dyslexic. Her history also demonstrated how quickly some people can learn to read and spell.

When comparing reading and spelling abilities with intellectual abilities I have stressed the need to use verbal reasoning skills as the basis for comparison. I'll explain why that is important. The most commonly used measure of intellectual ability in a diagnostic setting is the Wechsler Scales of Intellectual Abilities. There is a version for children and young teenagers (WISC), and a version for adults (WAIS). Each version consists of a series of subtests which are used to measure performance on a range of different skills including knowledge of vocabulary, mental arithmetic, three-dimensional thinking and speed of copying symbols. When all the scores are combined IQ can be calculated.

For someone who is dyslexic it is unwise to use an IQ figure as a point of comparison with reading and spelling. This is because, in virtually all cases of dyslexia, an IQ measure would hide very important variations such as just how good – or poor – someone is at certain kinds of activities. In most cases a typical dyslexic Wechsler profile reveals higher scores for verbal and visual reasoning than for short-term memory and speed of visual processing. When no specific learning difficulties are present the Wechsler profile will be fairly flat, not spiky.

Jane's spiky profile (see Figure 2.1) is typical of a dyslexic student in that she scored above average on verbal and visual reasoning skills and below average on working memory and processing speed. Whereas her Verbal Comprehension (verbal reasoning) and Perceptual Organisation (visual reasoning) scores put her in the top 20 per cent and top 23 per cent of the population respectively, her scores for Working Memory and Processing Speed put her in the bottom 9 per cent and 32 per cent respectively.

This type of variation is important as it helps to explain a number of everyday experiences (see Chapter 1). However, once these scores are combined, the variation is lost and a false picture emerges. If Jane's verbal IQ is calculated by combining her verbal reasoning and working memory scores, her verbal IQ score places her in the bottom 45 per cent of the population. This is a big drop from being in the top 20 per cent for verbal reasoning.

The same kind of thing happens if scores from the subtests of visual reasoning and processing speed are combined to calculate Jane's performance IQ. Whereas Jane's score for visual reasoning places her in the top

23 per cent of the population, her performance IQ pushes her down to the top 37 per cent. Finally, when verbal IQ and performance IQ are together used to calculate a general IQ score, Jane's IQ of 101 places her just above the midpoint of 100 for the population. As she is actually of 'high average' ability on tests of verbal and visual reasoning, her IQ score is not a fair reflection of her real abilities, nor does it reveal the barriers that prevent her from achieving her full potential.

Whereas Jane's level of verbal reasoning places her in the top 20 per cent of the population, her levels of reading and spelling put her in the bottom 10 per cent and 8 per cent respectively, differences of 70 and 72 percentile points. These are major discrepancies. However, if you just compare her reading with her IQ the discrepancy will be much smaller, just 40 percentile points.

It is important to note that it is the extent of the discrepancy between the scores for reading and verbal reasoning that is the key to arriving at a diagnosis of dyslexia, not the level of reading by itself. That is, it is not necessary to be really poor at reading to be diagnosed as being dyslexic. While I have met several students whose reading skills are so poor that they find travelling difficult because they cannot read the names of stations or roads, most students I see can read. Probably about 10 per cent choose to read for pleasure.

It is not true that dyslexics cannot read. Most can, but their reading ability is well below expectation. For example, I frequently see students whose performance on the assessment of verbal reasoning places them in the

top 1 per cent of the population. However, their reading
puts them in the bottom 30 per cent or 40 per cent
of the population. While it is the case that these
students can read some types of books and newspapers
with a fair degree of accuracy and fluency, their real
reading difficulties become apparent only when reading
academic books and research papers.

One student described how, when reading a novel,
she just 'flowed with the story' and skipped over words
she didn't recognise. However, when reading an
academic text, she had to read every word and
concentrate on remembering what she had just read.
Reading is not just a question of reading words with
accuracy. It is also being able to retain the information
and not be distracted while reading, both of which are
well known dyslexic features. Hannah's illustration
of herself 'reading' but not taking in what she is
reading captures this typical dyslexic challenge (see
Illustration 2.1). On top of this, visual stress may also
be present (see Chapter 6). It is important to remember
that reading is a multi-skilled process.

Because the profile of abilities for dyslexics is an
uneven one, some definitions of dyslexia state that, in
addition to an unexpected weakness in reading and
spelling, dyslexia is characterised by one or more
cognitive weaknesses as well. (Note. The word
'cognitive' just means a mental process carried out by
the brain, such as remembering.) This type of definition,
with its emphasis on information-processing, is the type
I favour, as it helps to focus attention on the complex
nature of dyslexia. Another general advantage of

Illustration 2.1

information-processing definitions is that they do not
usually specify which cognitive weakness, or weaknesses,
have to be present. This is important, for the reality
of dyslexia is that there are a variety of dyslexias,
not just one.

One of the most important books on dyslexia was
written over sixty years ago, by the English educational
psychologist Fred Schonell (1945). Schonell did not use
the term dyslexia as it was not in common use at that
time, but instead referred to 'backward readers and
spellers'. In his 1945 book he describes three different
patterns of reading difficulties. He points out that some
children, whom he called auditorily weak, have very
good visual recognition skills but poor phonological
skills. Others have the reverse profile. That is, visually
weak children have good phonological skills but are
poor at visual recognition. Yet others are poor at both
phonological processing and visual recognition.

Such differentiation is important in that good
phonological and visual skills are necessary to read well
in English. This is because English contains many
irregular words that are not spelt as they sound and so
do not follow the general phonetic spelling rules. When
words are regular they are easy to read and to pronounce
correctly, even if you have never encountered them
before.

For example, if you have good phonological skills you
will be able to read the sentence 'Zog norded nov
Mungent' with some fluency and accuracy. However,
when a word is irregular, it has to be recognised from
its shape. For example, the sentence 'The reigning

sovereign campaigned from her yacht' contains four irregular words. Those dyslexics with good visual recognition skills but poor phonological ones would be able to read 'The reigning sovereign campaigned from her yacht' with little difficulty, but would really struggle with 'Zog norded nov Mungent'.

Unlike English, a number of languages such as Italian and Spanish (but not Hispanic Spanish – that is, Spanish spoken in Latin America) are phonetically regular. A visually weak dyslexic Italian or Spanish person would not necessarily encounter major difficulties with learning to read or write in their own language. However, it is highly likely that the process of learning will be slow, for the other facets of dyslexia would still apply such as finding it hard to remember what they have just read, and daydreaming at school when they should be reading or listening to the teacher at school.

Maria is a classic example of a visually weak Spanish dyslexic. Her teachers and parents could never understand why she always performed badly in exams and homework at school when she had a very good vocabulary and her verbal skills were excellent. Reading in Spanish was not a problem for Maria and, when she lived at home, she read three to four books a month for pleasure. Maria had to learn English at school but because she found it so difficult her parents paid for her to visit the UK to practise. When Maria was 14 she had still not learnt all the times tables and her parents paid for her to have private maths tuition. She also had to repeat a year at high school. Her mother always complained about how disorganised Maria was.

Maria eventually enrolled, as a mature student, at an art college in the UK, which provided the opportunity for her to be assessed. This assessment revealed an excellent level of verbal comprehension but a very weak working memory. In addition, her short-term visual memory is also poor. (This means that when she looks at something and then looks away, her visual memory fades away much faster than would be expected.) Maria can read regularly spelt English words with virtually no problems. However, her error rate for irregular English words is nine times greater than for regular ones. That is, her memory for the shape of words is very poor.

If we define dyslexia as being an unexpected difficulty with acquiring reading skills, Maria is dyslexic when assessed on her reading in English but not dyslexic when assessed on her Spanish reading skills. However, her cognitive profile remains the same whether she is living in Spain or the UK, and her everyday experiences and behaviours are typical of dyslexia. By knowing about the different forms that dyslexia can take, it is possible to understand why this is so. This is why it is so important to realise that dyslexia is more than just an unexpected difficulty with reading. The underlying cognitive landscape differs from dyslexic to dyslexic.

This individual complexity is captured within the current British Dyslexia Association definition:

> Accompanying weaknesses may be identified in areas of speed of processing, short-term memory, organisation, sequencing, spoken language and

motor skills. There may be difficulties with auditory and/or visual perception.

(Tresman, 2006, page 7)

It is more than sixty years since Schonell first described three different subtypes of dyslexia. Since then there have been several more attempts to identify differing forms of dyslexia. For example, Elena Boder (1971) in the USA and Andrew Ellis (1984) in the UK each advanced the case for there being three types of dyslexia, but with little general success. Interestingly, the match between the subtypes proposed by Schonell, Ellis and Boder is a very close one, and some researchers (e.g. Ben-Yehudah et al., 2001), still take care to make use of these three general categories of dyslexia

Probably the reason why Schonell, Ellis and Boder enjoyed little practical recognition when they subdivided dyslexia into three subtypes is that, in practice, it is not always clear cut as to which category of dyslexia a person should be assigned to, and sometimes no category appears to be appropriate. This does not mean that we should therefore think of dyslexia as being a unitary concept. It is far more helpful to recognise that dyslexia is a combination of strengths and weaknesses, and that dyslexic profiles can often be quite different from each other in a number of ways, without having to worry about how many types of dyslexia there are. Nevertheless, it would be a major step forward if we spoke of 'the dyslexias', as this would at least draw attention to the need to think about the particular range of characteristics each individual has.

The advantage of using the Wechsler Scales of Intelligence as part of a diagnostic assessment is that, by plotting the four Index scores of Verbal Comprehension, Working Memory, Perceptual Organisation and Processing Speed, different profiles are revealed. Although Jane's double-spike profile is the one most commonly found in assessments, there are significant variations from this. For example, Figure 2.2 reveals that Juliette's performance on Perceptual Organisation (a measure of visual reasoning ability), as well as her Processing Speed score, are well above her Verbal Comprehension performance (a measure of verbal reasoning ability), while her score for Working Memory is particularly low.

Whereas her Processing Speed score (her highest score) places her in the top 10 per cent of the population, her Working Memory score puts her in the bottom 10 per cent.

Jason's profile (see Figure 2.3) is almost a mirror image of Juliette's. His Working Memory score is above average, and on a par with his Verbal Comprehension score. However, his Processing Speed score places him in the bottom 14 per cent. Interestingly, Jason's reading profile revealed he made five times as many errors when reading irregular words than regular ones, and his speed of reading was almost half that expected of an undergraduate. In many ways he is typical of the reader that Schonell identified as having poor visual word recognition skills but good phonological skills.

Jane, Juliette and Jason are all dyslexic in that all three have unexpected difficulties with reading and

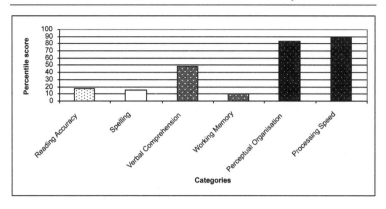

Figure 2.2 Juliette's Reading and Spelling scores, plus 4 WAIS-III Index scores expressed as percentile scores

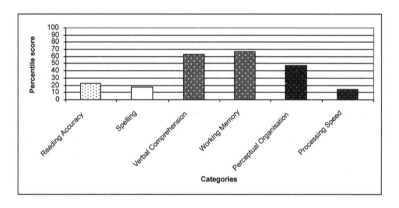

Figure 2.3 Jason's Reading and Spelling scores, plus 4 WAIS-III Index scores expressed as percentile scores

spelling. They all have one or more cognitive weaknesses as well as strengths. However, their cognitive profiles are significantly different, and these differences will be reflected in their everyday experiences. For example, Juliette is inclined to be impulsive and very forgetful, while Jason dislikes having to work under pressure and prefers to think carefully about his responses before answering questions. Because the factors underlying dyslexic cognitive profiles influence and colour such a wide range of everyday behaviours and experiences, it is more helpful to think of dyslexia as being a lifestyle – but a style that is for life.

Although the profile of a dyslexic person frequently reveals cognitive strengths and weaknesses, it is important to realise that these weaknesses are part of being dyslexic, but do not cause the dyslexia. The typical double spike observed for many dyslexics is often found in instances of dyspraxia and ADHD as well (see Chapters 3 and 4), even when reading and spelling are good. Very occasionally, this double-spike profile is observed when a person is neither dyslexic nor dyspraxic and does not have ADHD. In order to understand what dyslexia is, it is necessary to understand what lies beneath the profiles.

There has been no shortage of attempts to explain the basis of dyslexia. Currently there are four popular major theories. Rather than asking which one is right, I believe it is more helpful to think of them as providing different perspectives on what is a very complex neurological picture.

The word 'dyslexia' literally means difficulties with language, and was first coined about 130 years ago. There has always been debate about whether dyslexia is just a difficulty with language, or a mixture of verbal and visual components. Probably for the past twenty years the most popular theoretical explanation has been that dyslexia is the result of phonological processing difficulties.

The first name that comes to mind when this theory is mentioned is likely to be that of Professor Margaret Snowling. She claims: 'Dyslexia is a specific form of language impairment that affects the way the brain encodes the phonological features of spoken words. The core deficit is in phonological processing . . .' (Snowling, 2000, page 213). Phonological processing refers to the brain's ability to break down a stream of sounds into very small parts when listening to someone talk, and then recombine the units to make sense of what is being said. If there is a weakness in phonological processing, this will have an impact on a range of experiences.

For example, some dyslexics find it hard to follow a conversation in a noisy environment even though others have no such difficulty. Some confuse similar sounding words, such as 'specific' and 'Pacific', and 'divert' and 'diverse'. This phonological weakness also affects the ability to match the right letters to sounds when spelling. For example, an attempt to spell 'quarrel' might result in 'corral'. It will also affect the ability to learn how to break words down into their component sounds when learning to read, as well as the ability to remember verbal information for a short period of time. It is as if the brain is trying to remember and recall auditory information that is not very clear or well defined. This is why it can be difficult to hold information in working memory.

It may affect long-term memory as well for information has to be both stored and retrieved with precision. If the auditory sounds are slightly fuzzy it will take slightly longer to retrieve the information. Often someone will say that they know they know the answer to a question, but can't quite arrive at it on demand. This is sometimes called the 'tip-of-tongue' phenomenon.

A few psychologists have gone so far as to recommend that dyslexia be defined just as a weakness in phonological processing. They point out that by adopting this approach there is no longer a need to assess intellectual abilities. However, most psychologists and educationalists are wary of going down this path. Jane's profile shows that there are two key cognitive weaknesses associated with dyslexia, not one. In my experience, this double-spike profile is observed in about 80 per cent of dyslexics I have seen.

Jason is one of the 20 per cent of dyslexics without a double-spike profile. His profile is important because it reveals that there are some dyslexic people who do not have a weak working memory. This poses a problem for those who argue that phonological processing is the defining feature of dyslexia.

Another problem for the phonologists, as will be revealed in the next chapter, is that some dyspraxics have excellent reading and spelling skills but still have a weak working memory. If a difficulty with phonological processing results in problems with learning to read and spell, as well as with working memory, how can someone be good at reading but poor at remembering things for a short period of time? These questions remain unanswered.

While the work of Margaret Snowling is important, and has been very influential, the phonological deficit hypothesis is just one of several attempts to provide a causal explanation of the nature of dyslexia. Currently there are at least three other major theories offered as alternatives. The double deficit hypothesis proposed by Maryanne Wolf states that in addition to a phonological deficit, there is also a speed of processing deficit. This double deficit concept sits well with the double spike seen in most Wechsler profiles. However, as Juliette's profile reveals, not all dyslexics experience a problem with speed of timing. Once again, there are problems with trying to generalise about dyslexia.

Professor John Stein has developed quite a different theory – the magnocellular theory – to account for dyslexia. Central to this is the proposition that the brains of dyslexics have fewer magnocellular cells than those of non-dyslexics, especially in the pathway that conveys visual information from the eyes to the back of the brain and the specialised visual fields. The available evidence to date (e.g. Ramus et al., 2003) suggests that while this is probably true for some dyslexics, it does not hold true in all cases.

The fourth major hypothesis, often referred to as the cerebellum hypothesis, has been developed by Rod Nicolson and Angela Fawcett. In essence, they believe that the cerebellum – which plays a crucial role in integrating different streams of information as well as in relaying this information to the rest of the brain – may be underperforming in dyslexics. Because of this, learning takes longer. They also believe it accounts for poor balance in dyslexics. Once again, this theory is not without its critics (e.g. Ramus et al., 2003). There is evidence that some dyslexics have an underperforming cerebellum, but not all do. I am far from convinced that the cerebellum hypothesis applies universally to all dyslexics, since the proportion of dyslexics who excel at sports is relatively high (see Chapter 8).

Having met dyslexics who are national champions at ice-skating, cycling and gymnastics – all sports that require excellent balance – a difficulty with balance is not a universal dyslexic trait. I believe, however, that it is possible to reconcile these very different approaches. Fundamental to all of them is some form of weakness in information processing. It is possible that this occurs at a very basic level.

For information processing to take place, incoming streams of information have to be broken down into small bits of information, which are then reassembled to give them meaning. For example, when listening to someone talking, it is as if the brain breaks the continuous stream of information down into small chunks of information every 130 milliseconds. However, there is some evidence that in cases of dyslexia the chunks are larger – perhaps about 210 milliseconds in length (Helenius et al., 1999). There may also be a similar type of difference in visual processing. It has been shown that, at the first memory stage of visual information processing, the time it takes for an image to decay and disappear, which is usually just milliseconds, is shorter for dyslexics (Ben-Yehudah et al., 2001). As the very brief visual images decay faster than expected, this results in the brain experiencing some difficulties with comparing the last image with the current one. It's as if the picture is slightly cloudy.

Although these four major theories about dyslexia appear at first sight to be quite different from each other, there is one theory which can unite all of them – the asynchrony hypothesis of Michel Habib (2000). A significant feature of Habib's way of thinking about dyslexia is that it encompasses dyspraxia as well. His ideas about the underlying basis of dyslexia are important, for he has proposed that the tempo of information processing may be different in dyslexics.

If we assume that the brain works best when all neuronal systems are in synchrony with each other, difficulties will arise if one system is running very fast or very slow compared with the others. There are many different systems in the brain, including the major ones of vision, language and movement. If the time-coding of information processing is impaired between these three systems, then both dyslexia and dyspraxia are likely.

If just one system is affected it might give rise to a visual or verbal form of dyslexia. In principle, it is possible to see how slow timing in one system gives rise to difficulties when integration between systems is required. If the auditory timing is slow, then the matching of sounds with images will be problematic and will result in slowness with some forms of learning.

The concept of processing systems needing to run at 'the right pace', as it were, also applies to the creation of memories. For memories to become permanent it is necessary for the nerve cells of the brain to fire at the right tempo and in the right sequence (Fields, 2005).

If visual or auditory processing systems are not operating at the same rate – that is, they are asynchronous – this is likely to have a knock-on effect in that long-term memory is also affected.

It appears to me that Habib's approach not only encompasses all four of the current major theories of dyslexia, but also goes beyond them since it embraces dyspraxia as well as dyslexia. What most theorists overlook is that dyslexia and dyspraxia are not separate conditions. I have found that about 25 per cent of the students I see are dyslexic and dyspraxic – to differing degrees. Many experts on dyspraxia claim that the overlap is even higher. Because there is such an overlap, I suggest that we can only claim to understand what dyslexia is when that explanation encompasses dyspraxia as well.

Bibliography

Ben-Yehudah, G., Sackett, E., Malchi-Ginzberg, L. & Ahissar, M. (2001) 'Impaired temporal contrast sensitivity in dyslexics is specific to retain-and-compare paradigms', *Brain*, 124, 1381–1395.

Boder, E. (1971) 'Developmental dyslexia: A diagnostic screening procedure based on three characteristic patterns of reading and spelling'. In Bateman, B. (ed.) *Learning Disorders*, 4, Special Children Publications, Seattle.

Ellis, A.W. (1984) *Reading, Writing and Dyslexia: A Cognitive Analysis*, Lawrence Erlbaum Associates, NJ.

Fawcett, A.J. & Nicolson, R. (2004) 'Dyslexia: the role of the cerebellum'. In Reid, G. & Fawcett, A. (eds) *Dyslexia in Context: Research, Policy and Practice*, Whurr Publishers, London.

Fields, R.D. (2005) 'Making memories stick', *Scientific American*, 292, 2, 59–65.

Habib, M. (2000) 'The neurological basis of developmental dyslexia: An overview and working hypothesis', *Brain*, 123, 2373–2399.

Helenius, P., Uutela, K. & Hari, R. (1999) 'Auditory stream segregation in dyslexic adults', *Brain*, 122, 907–913.

Ramus, F., Rosen, S., Dakin, S.C., Day, B.L., Castellote, J.M., White, S. & Frith, U. (2003) 'Theories of developmental dyslexia: insights from a multiple case study of dyslexic adults', *Brain*, 126, 841–865.

Schonell, F.J. (1945) *Backwardness in the Basic Subjects*, 2nd edition, Oliver & Boyd Ltd., Edinburgh and London.

Snowling, M.J. (2000) *Dyslexia*, 2nd edition, Blackwell Publishers, Oxford.

Stein, J., Talcott, J. & Witton, C. (2001) 'The sensorimotor basis of developmental dyslexia'. In Fawcett, A. (ed.) *Dyslexia: Theory and Good Practice*, Whurr Publishing, London.

Tresman, S. (2006) 'What is dyslexia?' In Tresman, S. & Cooke, A. (eds) *The Dyslexia Handbook*, British Dyslexia Association, Reading.

Wolf, M. & O'Brien, B. (2001) 'On issues of time, fluency, and intervention'. In Fawcett, A. (ed.) *Dyslexia: Theory and Good Practice*, Whurr Publishing, London.

Further reading

Moody, S. (2007) *Dyslexia: Surviving and Succeeding at College*, Routledge, Oxford.

Chapter 3

What is dyspraxia?

When carrying out a diagnostic assessment I always ask the question: 'Were you well coordinated or clumsy as a child?' In a surprisingly high number of cases the reply is: 'I was clumsy – still am.' Clumsiness and difficulties with motor coordination are classic soft signs of the presence of dyspraxia. When these difficulties are severe enough to result in a clumsy child being diagnosed as being dyspraxic, a physiotherapist or occupational therapist will then work with that child to bring about improvements in motor coordination. In some cases speech therapy is required as well. However, it is a mistake to assume that improvements in motor control and speech result in a 'cure' for dyspraxia. The underlying cognitive characteristics, a big part of being dyspraxic, are still very much the same and are often ignored. In addition, many people are never diagnosed as being dyspraxic in the first place. For example, Laura has lived with being clumsy throughout her life but has just accepted this as being part of her: 'I have learnt to live with who I am.'

Dyspraxia is similar to an iceberg in two ways. First, there is a small visible part with a very considerable hidden portion. The visible part in the case of dyspraxia is the element of clumsiness and associated difficulties with motor coordination. The hidden aspect is the underlying difficulties with attention, memory and some tasks requiring perceptual skills. The second similarity is that, over time, the visible part becomes smaller and less noticeable. This gradual melting away analogy refers to the observation that coordination skills improve over time and people also learn to become 'more careful'. Consequently, as a child grows into a teenager and then an adult, the visible aspects of being dyspraxic often become quite muted. However, and crucially, the underlying cognitive picture changes very little.

The most obvious aspect of being dyspraxic is clumsiness, and this is summed up in the phrase 'clumsy child syndrome'. Clumsiness can take different forms, such as bumping into things, knocking things over, spilling things, and tripping over your own feet. As it is demeaning, as well as age-inappropriate, to refer to a teenager or adult who is clumsy as having clumsy child syndrome, the term 'dyspraxic' is much more frequently used.

Within recent years there has been a move to rename dyspraxia as Developmental Coordination Disorder (e.g. Drew, 2005). I have considerable difficulties with accepting this change as one for the better because the defining criteria are taken from the *Diagnosis and Statistical Manual of Mental Disorders*, 4th edition (DSM-IV), of the American Psychiatric Association, and they make no reference to the cognitive profile of dyspraxia. DCD (Developmental Coordination Disorder) is defined in terms of 'a marked impairment in motor coordination'. In addition, I am uneasy with dyspraxia being defined by psychiatrists. Dyspraxia is not a mental disorder.

As a consequence of my unhappiness with the attempt to rename dyspraxia as Developmental Coordination Disorder I have developed, with help from others, a new definition of dyspraxia. The short version is given below. The fuller version is given at the end of this chapter.

> Dyspraxia is present when a motor coordination weakness, frequently expressed as clumsiness, in combination with significant variations in neurocognitive function, impact in a noticeable way on everyday life. Dyspraxia is thus an umbrella term for it varies in form and severity. Motor coordination weaknesses may be primarily of fine motor control, gross motor control, or both. Significant variations in neurocognitive function typically include weaknesses in visual processing speed, short-term visual memory, implicit memory processing, and short-term auditory memory (i.e. working memory). In many instances, but not all, verbal conceptual understanding and verbal knowledge are noticeably better than visual reasoning and spatial abilities. In a minority of instances mathematical skills are exceptionally strong.

As with dyslexia, I believe it is more helpful to talk about the dyspraxias than dyspraxia because it can take different forms. However, rather than worry about how many labels there should be, I believe it is much more important to focus on the profile of an individual's strengths and weaknesses. In my view, the use of the Wechsler Intelligence Scales is essential to drawing up that profile. This battery of tests can bring into full view many of the hidden aspects of dyspraxia.

This point can be illustrated by describing two students I have seen. John was first diagnosed as being dyspraxic when he was 7. Amanda was not diagnosed as being dyspraxic until she was in her early twenties. John's birth was a very difficult one, and he was a floppy baby (rather like a rag doll – his legs and arms flopped about). He had not stood up by the time he was 18 months old and was provided with physiotherapy to help him learn to walk. He was also a very messy eater. Although he was walking by the time he started school he could not climb steps and was consequently provided with further physiotherapy. It was not until he was 7 that a consultant finally diagnosed him as being dyspraxic. What is striking about John's case is how long it took for his parents to be given a diagnosis. As this can take so long even when motor coordination difficulties are evident from so early on, it is easy to understand why children with more subtle forms of coordination difficulties are not identified at all.

When I met John he was studying English literature at a highly respected university. His assessment (see Figure 3.1) revealed a very high level of verbal reasoning ability – top 0.1 per cent of the population. His visual reasoning abilities, although 'high average',

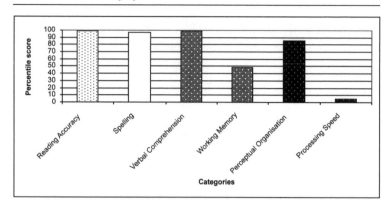

Figure 3.1 John's Reading and Spelling scores, plus 4 WAIS-III Index scores expressed as percentile scores

are well below his exceptionally high verbal reasoning performance. Of the three visual reasoning subtests he took, his lowest score was on the Block Design subtest, a test of being able to think three-dimensionally. A dip in performance on this subtest is a typical dyspraxic feature. There is a working memory weakness and John's speed of visual processing is exceptionally low – bottom 5 per cent of the population.

Although John's visual reasoning performance is comfortably above average, his sense of place and space is nevertheless very poor. It takes him very much longer than most people to learn how to find his way around a building or area, and he still gets lost in places he has known for some time. John is prone to lapses in concentration and his writing style is typically dyslexic, in that he finds it hard to structure essays and writes sentences that are very long and complex, with poor punctuation. This is in spite of his having excellent skills of spelling and word reading accuracy. His reading speed is a little below average. As with most dyspraxics his handwriting speed is very slow and, when writing, he experiences pain in his hand after just a short period of time. As a child John experienced some difficulties with learning to read, and he disliked having to read aloud in secondary school as he had some problems with pronunciation. He has always found it hard to get to sleep.

Many of John's experiences are common to dyslexia and constitute part of the hidden side of dyspraxia. Until his assessment John had not been aware that these experiences are dyspraxia-related. However, they directly reflect his cognitive weaknesses in working memory, visual processing speed and short-term visual memory. Like many dyspraxics students I have seen, John's level of verbal reasoning is exceptionally high. John's difficulties with motor coordination were clearly evident from his earliest months. Amanda's difficulties were more muted. There are many similarities between John and Amanda. Their WAIS profiles are very similar, except that Amanda scored lower on Working Memory (see Figure 3.2). Like John, her word reading accuracy and spelling skills are excellent, whereas her speed of reading is below average.

Amanda was a 'blue' baby and began walking a little late. She was always 'bumping into lamp-posts' as a child, and still bumps into people. She disliked sports at school because she could not catch or throw. She tried to learn a number of musical instruments but eventually settled on the flute because it required less coordination than the guitar or piano. Amanda took a degree in life

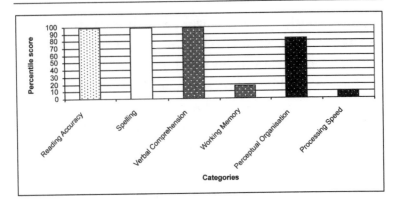

Figure 3.2 Amanda's Reading and Spelling scores, plus 4 WAIS-III Index scores expressed as percentile scores

sciences but struggled with some of the practical activities such as drawing while using a microscope, and with titration. (This activity requires a flask to be swirled with one hand and a tap turned on and off, quite gently but swiftly, with the other.) Amanda has always learnt slowly, especially when rote learning was required, and she chose options on her degree that were coursework-based, even though it took her longer than other students to write essays and reports. In order to be organised she has to write herself lists of things to do. She is easily distracted when engaged in activities such as reading or writing.

Although Amanda initially sought an assessment because of the study difficulties she was experiencing, the more subtle problems she had with motor coordination only came to light when she was asked a series of questions about her personal history. Amanda's case is important since it raises the serious question of whether dyspraxia is the appropriate diagnosis for her.

If the DSM-IV standard is followed, then such a diagnosis can only be applied when there is a marked impairment in motor coordination and this has a significant adverse effect on academic achievement or the activities of daily life. The DSM-IV approach avoids saying anything about other associated aspects, such as weaknesses in memory, attention and perception.

Although Amanda's difficulties with motor coordination are not marked, they have had an impact on a range of activities, such as avoiding having to take part in sports, influencing which musical instrument she could learn, and asking her university laboratory partner to carry out titrations on her behalf. She has genuine continuing difficulties with coordination but, compared with John's, they are muted. They are also much less obvious as she has learnt to be more careful. On the other hand, her cognitive profile is a very spiky one, and this has impacted negatively on her experiences at school and university, and colours her everyday life. Because my definition is more holistic than the DSM-IV approach in that it captures the cognitive as well as the motor coordination aspects of being dyspraxic, the most appropriate diagnosis for Amanda is dyspraxia. Amanda is typical of many who have been affected by dyslexic-type experiences without being dyslexic, and not known why school, university and work have posed so many challenges.

Whereas John's and Amanda's profiles are very similar in many ways, there are other types of profiles. The profile for Cathy (see Figure 3.3) is one also typically encountered in instances of dyspraxia. The most obvious difference from the profiles of John and Amanda is that Cathy's performance on visual reasoning is below average, and is on a par with her score for speed of visual processing. (In my experience, a low score on Perceptual Organisation is often associated with difficulties with maths, and Cathy required three attempts before she passed a national maths exam.)

Cathy's birth was free of complications. She recalled always dropping things as a child and, as an adult, she has a tendency to bump into things. She struggled with learning handwriting skills and tying her shoelaces, and she still has trouble with zips and putting on make-up, especially nail varnish. Cathy is accident prone and broke her arm and her leg in separate accidents in her teens. To date she has also broken either three or four mobile phones through dropping them, and permanently lost several phones as well.

When Cathy was at secondary school she was placed in the top groups for all subjects except needlework.

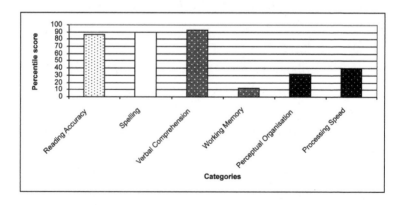

Figure 3.3 Cathy's Reading and Spelling scores, plus 4 WAIS-III Index scores expressed as percentile scores

Cathy said she was unable to thread a needle. Her school would not let her enter a national art exam. Cathy recalled forgetting to take items she needed to school, and her teachers often mentioned that her written work was poor in terms of planning and punctuation. Her difficulty with organising ideas when writing essays became so debilitating that, although Cathy completed first a degree and then a masters course, she felt that her 'academic self-confidence' had been destroyed. It was not until she had a diagnostic assessment that, for the first time, she was able to understand why she had consistently underperformed throughout her education, and was able to make sense of her everyday experiences.

All three case studies reveal that being dyspraxic affects more than just motor coordination. It is, like dyslexia, a complex neuropsychological profile of significant variations in strengths and weaknesses. Because there are so many shared similarities it is not surprising that, in my experience at least, I record the present of dyspraxia in about 25 per cent of individuals who are dyslexic.

As with cases of undiagnosed dyslexia, the constant struggle to achieve at school and university can erode self-confidence. Even skills that dyspraxics become good at, such as reading and spelling, often take them longer than others to learn. In many cases being poor at sports further erodes self-confidence, particularly if this is accompanied by bullying. The case histories of Amanda and Cathy are typical of many dyspraxics I see in that their difficulties with motor coordination are not sufficiently severe for a clinical opinion to be sought. There are times when you wonder just how severe this has to be. For example, I have spoken to one student who was only referred for a clinical opinion when his infant school teacher recognised that his constant falling off his chair at school was due to lack of motor control.

Nevertheless, the signs of problems with motor coordination were plainly evident from childhood and have shaped their lives. Being dyspraxic, even when the motor elements are relatively muted, does affect lives and influence career choices. For example, only about 5 per cent of dyspraxic students I see are studying art and design. However, of the students I see from what are regarded as the UK's top universities, a third are dyspraxic. Intuitively you would expect that dyspraxic students would experience some difficulties with art and design type subjects. As they often have very considerable verbal skills, and in many cases good or excellent mathematical skills, it could be anticipated that dyspraxics are more likely to choose to study such subjects as the humanities and sciences at university.

In comparison with dyslexia, dyspraxia is grossly under-researched. It is my opinion that the underlying causal mechanisms are the same or similar to those encountered in dyslexia. However, the trigger in many cases appears to be a difficult birth: about 60 to 70 per cent of dyspraxics seen by myself report there were birthing complications of one kind or another, such as a forceps delivery following a long and difficult labour, an emergency Caesarean section, or being born prematurely. It is possible that the neurological processes serving working memory and processing speed are particularly vulnerable to factors that stress the brain, such as a difficult labour. It is known that closed brain injuries, such as occur following a motor car crash, affect both working memory and processing speed. This points towards the relative fragility of these neurological systems. There is also evidence that when the brain is subjected to stress, right hemisphere functions are affected more greatly than left hemisphere ones. The higher score for verbal than visual reasoning often observed in many cases of dyspraxia is indicative of a stronger left hemisphere.

In conclusion, there are probably even more unanswered questions about the dyspraxias than there are about the dyslexias. What we can be sure of is that the defining feature of dyspraxia – difficulty with motor coordination – is the tip of the iceberg. Psychologists need to work in conjunction in physiotherapists and occupational therapists to ensure that dyspraxics are given access to the full, complex picture.

Definition

I first presented a draft of the definition below at a DANDA (Developmental Adult Neuro-Diversity Association) workshop in November 2008, on the assessment of dyspraxia and ADHD. Following feedback from participants and some DANDA members the draft has evolved to the one presented below. It has since entered the public domain and may be freely quoted in its entirety:

Dyspraxia is present when a motor coordination weakness, frequently expressed as clumsiness, in combination with significant variations in neurocognitive function, impact in a noticeable way on everyday life. Dyspraxia is thus an umbrella term for it varies in form and severity. Motor coordination weaknesses may be primarily of fine motor control, gross motor control, or both. They are reflected in a range of everyday experiences, including bumping into objects and people, poor balance, stumbling, dropping items (such as mobile phones and remote controls), knocking objects over and spilling things.

Many, but not all, individuals who are dyspraxic experience significant difficulties with such everyday tasks as cleaning and cooking, folding clothes neatly, putting on make-up, DIY and craft activities, learning to drive, using a computer keyboard and mouse, and handwriting.

Significant variations in neurocognitive function typically include weaknesses in visual processing speed, short-term visual memory, implicit memory processing, and short-term auditory memory (i.e. working memory). In many instances, but not all, verbal conceptual understanding and verbal knowledge are noticeably better than visual reasoning and spatial abilities.

These neurocognitive weaknesses are reflected in such everyday experiences as forgetfulness, disorganisation, (including difficulties with time management and sequencing), going off at tangents, slowness at learning the spatial layout of a new environment or building, and assimilating a large body of information quickly. There are frequently strengths in verbal knowledge and conceptual understanding. However, speed of speech production is sometimes relatively slow and, occasionally, pronunciation difficulties are sufficiently severe to justify a diagnosis of verbal dyspraxia. In some instances the 'reading' of non-verbal face and body signs may be relative weak. In a minority of instances mathematical skills are exceptionally strong.

Dyspraxia is sometimes accompanied by other specific learning differences such as ADHD, dyslexia, dysorthographia, a specific maths weakness and Asperger's Syndrome. The particular combination of dyspraxia and ADHD is sometimes referred to as DAMP (Disorders of Attention, Motor control and Perception).

Dyspraxia occurs as frequently in females as males and there is sometimes a family history of dyspraxia. Birthing difficulties, such as prematurity (including early prematurity), or a long and difficult labour are frequently reported. Some dyspraxics are hyper-sensitive to touch, sound or light, and many report sleep difficulties.

Improvements in motor coordination can and do occur over time, especially when appropriate physical activities are undertaken. However, the under-lying neurocognitive profile is less subject to change, with the consequence that while early motor difficulties are often more muted in adults with dyspraxia, everyday activities that are dependent on basic cognitive processes are still affected.

It is only when motor coordination difficulties are *not* accompanied by significant variation in neurocognitive function that it is appropriate to use the diagnosis term 'developmental co-ordination disorder'.

David Grant, January, 2009

Bibliography

Drew, S. (2005) *Developmental Co-ordination Disorders in Adults*, Whurr Publishers Ltd., West Sussex.

Further reading

Colley, M. (2006) *Living with Dyspraxia: A Guide for Adults with Developmental Dyspraxia*, revised edition, Jessica Kingsley Publishing, London.

Chapter 4

What is ADHD?

I need freedom, but not too much freedom.

When I met Holly she was a failing research student. The difficulties she was encountering surprised both Holly and her supervisors. Before starting her three-year independent research programme she had been a straight A student throughout the first four years of her medical degree. Because she was judged to be very academically able she was invited to complete her medical degree by becoming a research student. Her first research task was to read all the relevant journal papers, write them up as a summary, and identify the theme she wished to research in depth. She failed badly in this task. When I met Holly she said her major problem with undertaking the necessary reading and writing was procrastination: 'I invented procrastination.'

Holly described how, when she sat down in front of her computer to start writing, she would inevitably start engaging in other activities: 'I might suddenly realise I hadn't checked my text messages recently so I would get my mobile phone out. I might then wonder why I hadn't heard from Joan recently. This would remind me of the last meal we had together a couple of weeks ago and I would then start thinking about what I might have to eat this evening. So I would leave my computer to check what was in the fridge. On realising I was short of milk I would set off to the corner shop to get some. By this time my good intentions to spend the afternoon writing had been totally forgotten.'

Holly's difficulties with deciding which tasks to prioritise, and then ensuring she stayed focused on these tasks until they had been completed, was not fully evident until she began her research programme. Prior to that she had enjoyed what Tom Brown (2005) refers to as 'scaffolding' throughout her time at school and early years in medical school. That is, she had enjoyed a high degree of family and teacher support and encouragement to complete assignments on time and focus on her academic work. As a consequence of this constant support, Holly's underlying time management difficulties and short attention span remained masked throughout her childhood and teenage years. That is, she had some freedom, but not too much.

As an undergraduate medical student there had been the constant pressure of frequent deadlines for exams and in-class tests, and lots of multiple-choice questions. Holly is intellectually very able and understands complex ideas quite quickly so, at school in particular, she had achieved A grades with little effort. This meant she could put off revising until the very last minute. By choosing to study science and maths subjects, Holly avoided having to write lots of essays and undertake extended reading. Holly pointed out she finds it particularly hard to read long books as she is very easily distracted and loses concentration quickly, and every time she sits down to write an essay she finds something more interesting to do. Holly's very high level of intellectual ability also meant she was often bored in school lessons and her teachers frequently told her off for daydreaming. It was not until the 'scaffolding' of family and teaching support was finally removed, when she embarked on an independent research programme, that Holly's attentional difficulties became clearly visible – she now had 'too much freedom'. She was not hyperactive or impulsive, so her Attention Deficit Disorder (ADD) would not have become apparent to her family or teachers for a number of years.

In contrast with Holly, Emma's ADHD (Attention Deficit Hyperactivity Disorder) was evident from a very young age. Even as a small child she was 'always on the go' and her parents had trouble getting her to bed on time. Even as an adult she still has problems falling asleep, 'my brain is always excited' (see Illustration 4.1). Emma was very keen on taking part in sports at school and was, at various times, a member of many different teams. She described how she would take up a new sport 'with a burst of enthusiasm'. However, when she ran into difficulties with improving her skill level for a sport, 'I became frustrated, lost interest, and took up another sport. I have tried everything once.'

Emma became disenchanted with school at the age of 14 as she was 'not being stretched'. She left school at 15 and was pregnant when she was 16. Since then she has

Illustration 4.1

constantly moved from job to job and has also, at various times, set up her own business only to see it fail on each occasion. Emma explained that she is very good at problem-solving but very poor at maintaining discipline over a period of time, such as managing cash flow, paying bills on time and undertaking stock control. She also described herself finding it easy to initiate relationships but much harder to maintain them. Consequently she has experienced a number of failed close relationships.

It was only when Emma became a student in her mid-thirties that she was diagnosed as having (Attention Deficit Hyperactivity Disorder (ADHD). Her life history reveals a high element of risk-taking, failure to switch attention to tasks that need doing (e.g. paying bills on time), boundless energy, and periods when she would be hyper-focused on a task, such as setting up a new business, followed by a switch of focus when something else grabbed her attention. These are all typical signs of the presence of ADHD. Emma has long been aware her behaviour is different from that of others, and this had given rise to bouts of depression because she could not understand why things went wrong so frequently for her. This is a common experience for many individuals with ADHD, so it is no surprise that the incidence of mental health problems, such as depression and obsessive-compulsive behaviour, is higher when ADHD is present than for individuals with other specific learning differences (e.g. Brown, 2005).

Attention-Deficit Hyperactivity Disorder takes a number of different forms. Emma's is known as Attention-Deficit Hyperactivity Disorder (usually abbreviated to ADHD), whereas Holly's takes the form known as Attention-Deficit Disorder (ADD). (For the convenience of the reader I have used the acronym ADHD as shorthand for both ADD and ADHD. Although Hyperactivity frequently refers to the presence of both hyperactivity and impulsivity, it also covers the variants of ADD with impulsivity but no hyperactivity, and ADD with hyperactivity but no impulsivity. While the term ADDer is used by some individuals with a diagnosis of ADHD, not all are comfortable with describing themselves as ADDers, so it has not been used in this book.) The formal linking of attentional difficulties with hyperactivity is a relatively recent one, dating from 1987 (Brown, 2005). However, there is an increasing awareness that by defining ADHD in terms of inattention, there is a real danger that sight will be lost of the cognitive complexity of ADHD. As with dyslexia and dyspraxia, a spiky cognitive profile that varies from individual to individual, is often observed with ADHD, with the consequence that ADHD takes a variety of different forms.

Surprising as it may seem, one key feature associated with about one-third of individuals with ADHD I have seen has been almost completely overlooked. That is the presence of synaesthesia. Rhonda is a music student who has ADHD. Her ADHD takes the form of impulsivity without hyperactivity. She is also an individual with synaesthesia and a high level of visualisation. (Note. Visualisation and synaesthesia are covered in greater detail in Chapter 5.) In some key ways Rhonda is very like Emma. Just as Emma has taken up a wide range of sports, successively dropping one for the next, so Rhonda had taken up a series of musical instruments as her interest in each wanes in turn: 'My room is a graveyard for musical instruments.' Rhonda described herself as someone who makes constant changes, 'changes of various jobs, change of musical instruments, even appearance. People often say to me you have changed your hair-style, your hair colour yet again.' However, there are also some crucial differences between Rhonda and Emma. Rhonda is not hyperactive, but she is both dyslexic and a synaesthete.

There is nothing unusual about ADHD occurring together with dyslexia, for ADHD occurs more frequently in combination with another specific learning difference than in isolation (e.g. Hallowell & Ratey, 1995; Brown,

2005). This may be a key reason why the presence of attentional difficulties is so often overlooked, for the most prominent signs of the presence of a specific learning difference may be those of dyslexia or dyspraxia. About 40 per cent of the dyspraxic individuals I see also have ADHD. This link between ADHD and dyspraxia is so strong that some have argued (e.g. Gillberg & Kadesjö, 2003) the combination should be known as DAMP (Deficits in Attention, Motor control and Perception). However, a note of caution is required for occasionally I have concluded that, for some individuals with ADHD, their clumsiness appears to be linked with inattention and impulsivity, and is not due to poor motor coordination.

In my experience, dyslexia is found less frequently alongside ADHD. For example, Brown (2009) has reported that 25 per cent of individuals with ADHD are dyslexic, a figure that accords well with my own data. Rhonda had been referred for a diagnostic assessment as her music tutors suspected her difficulties with sight-reading music might be due to the presence of dyslexia. When asked how many books she had read for pleasure from cover to cover Rhonda replied 'about six or seven'. However, whilst Rhonda's dislike of reading is a sign of dyslexia, some individuals with ADHD also report difficulties with reading, due to an inability to concentrate for long. Rhonda not only found it hard to stay focused when reading, but also to remember what she had just read. Her personal history revealed many other instances of memory problems, such as remembering lyrics. As she was a singer this was a particular problem for her. Her difficulties with learning a foreign language at school resurfaced when she was assigned a part in an opera and asked to sing in Italian or German. As a child she struggled with learning the times tables, and as a student with remembering what had just been said in a lecture.

Rhonda's difficulties with remembering are not surprising, for many people with ADHD report problems with memory, and this is clearly reflected in their cognitive profile. For example, Brown (2009) and Bourne (2009) have both reported a spiky profile for those with ADHD, with strengths in verbal and visual reasoning but weaknesses in working memory and speed of processing. This profile is very similar to that often observed for dyslexics and dyspraxics. However, it is important to note that both Brown's and Bourne's observations are based on the profile for an average individual with ADHD. The danger with using an average is that it masks individual variation. In my experience this variation can be quite substantial.

Rhonda described herself as being 'very forgetful'. Even though she makes herself lists of things to do, she sometimes loses them. She is also prone to misplacing and losing items and estimated she has lost three mobile phones to date. Whilst Rhonda's everyday experiences point towards a working memory weakness, her performance on the three tests of working memory, taken as part of her diagnostic assessment, was better than expected (see Figure 4.2). However, her test scores are very misleading, as Rhonda's visualisation ability combined with her synaesthesia provides her with a way of remembering visually.

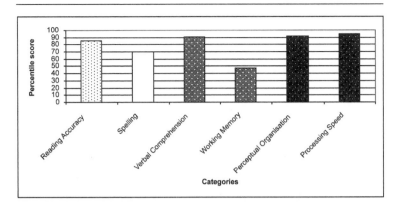

Figure 4.1 Emma's Reading and Spelling scores, plus 4 WAIS-III Index scores expressed as percentile scores

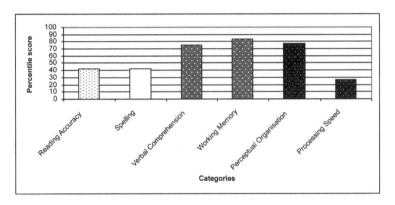

Figure 4.2 Rhonda's Reading and Spelling scores, plus 4 WAIS-III Index scores expressed as percentile scores

When asked to remember a series of letters Rhonda said she could not only 'see' them all, but each had its own colour. For example, *r* was red, *h* was yellow, *i* was grey and *o* was blue/green. This strong letter–colour association is a synaesthetic experience, that is, a blending of two different senses – in this case sound with vision. Rhonda's grapheme-colour synaesthesia also influenced the colour of words, with each word taking on the colour of its first letter. For example, she 'saw' her name as being coloured red.

Rhonda could also 'see' a series of numbers when they were read out. In this case they were all the same colour, blue. As a consequence of being able to visualise numbers and her letter–colour synaesthesia, when Rhonda was tested on her ability to remember numbers and letters with numbers, she could just read back what she was 'seeing' and did not need to rely on auditory memory. This combination of sensory abilities enabled her to achieve quite high scores on these two tests, which enhanced her Working Memory score. Without being aware that Rhonda's Working Memory score is a reflection of her reliance on visual rather than auditory memory, her Index figure for Working Memory would be mistakenly interpreted as meaning no memory difficulty is present when, in fact, there is quite a significant short-term auditory memory weakness. Unlike Emma's and Ali's WAIS-III profiles (see Figures 4.1 and 4.3), which clearly reveal the presence of a working memory weakness, Rhonda's profile (Figure 4.2) could easily be mistaken as showing an excellent auditory working memory ability.

Rhonda's synaesthesia also extends to days of the week. For example, she 'sees' *Monday* as red, *Wednesday* as green, *Friday* as blue, and *Sunday* as yellow. However, she also 'sees' her music modules as coloured (e.g. *Critical Theory* is blue, *Composing* is red), so Rhonda sometimes becomes confused when deciding what she needs to take with her to music college: 'Is red/blue (*Monday* and *Critical Theory*) the same as blue/red (*Critical Theory* on

Monday), or is blue Friday, which means it's red for Composing?' Rhonda's visualisation extends to playing and listening to music, in that each note in a scale has a particular shape. When playing a piece of music or singing, she 'sees' each shape and then converts it into its note. This causes problems when Rhonda is asked to improvise using just five notes from a scale, as she then finds it difficult to ignore the other notes/shapes in that scale.

About one in 25 of the general population is a synaesthete. My own research has revealed that about one in three individuals with ADHD are synaesthetes. This is a very high frequency and has a number of implications for understanding both the nature of the ADHD experience and ADHD itself. Visualisation is a common experience reported by many people (see Chapter 5). However, it varies enormously in its vividness and complexity. For a small but significant minority of people with ADHD, visualisation can be so powerful that it generates sensory overload. That is, when reading or taking part in a conversation, each word triggers an image or series of images, with the consequence that the focus of attention constantly flickers between trying to listen to what is being said and the stream of images: 'There are so many things at the same time it is very exhausting.'

Ali's visualisation was particularly complex and vivid, since 'each sound has its shape'. For example, the sound of a plane resulted in an image of 'particles, like smoke, flying everywhere', while the word Monday was a silver-coloured circle, Wednesday was a green tick and Friday white and rectangular. In spite of his visualisation and synaesthesia, Ali performed very badly on tests of Working Memory (see Figure 4.3) as his mental images of numbers and letters faded too quickly for him to make use of them. However, his lack of working memory capacity meant that he was very reliant on visual memory for both understanding and remembering: 'It is only when I have a complete picture I can understand.'

Like the 90 per cent of the synaesthetes I see, Ali had not realised his sensory experiences were in any way unusual and consequently had never discussed them with anyone else. This may be one reason why visualisation and synaesthesia have been overlooked by virtually all ADHD researchers, even though Lynn Weiss, who has ADHD, provides several vivid examples in her book on ADHD and creativity (1997) of how important visualisation is for her: 'I "see" the answer played out on the inner screen of my mind' (page 2).

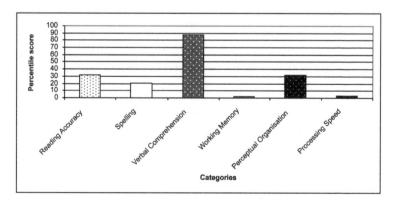

Figure 4.3 Ali's Reading and Spelling scores, plus 4 WAIS-III Index scores expressed as percentile scores

Visualisation and synaesthesia are not causes of ADHD. I believe, however, they offer clues to the nature of ADHD. I am in agreement with Tom Brown (2005) that ADHD is the consequence of the underperformance of different components of the brain's executive management system. (Note. While the executive management system is more complex that the executive system that controls working memory, two of its key components are working memory and processing speed.) However, I have been struck by the disparity between what would appear to be a mild working memory weakness when looking at a profile and that individual's account of him/herself. It is as if the presence of ADHD accentuates forgetfulness, a process I refer to in Chapter 1 as slipperiness. This may reflect the difficulties experienced by the executive management systems with inhibiting irrelevant thoughts.

It is easy to forget that while focusing on a particular task the brain is still monitoring many other cognitive processes simultaneously, many of which are running in an automatic or semi-automatic mode. For example, texting while walking with a group of friends involves thinking about what to say, how to say it, and which keys to press in which sequence. At the same time there is a monitoring of the environment to avoid bumping into things or people, or tripping over. Sounds will also be simultaneously monitored for traffic and conversation. There will also be a constant monitoring of emotional states, such as happiness, anxiety and fear. The executive management system has to decide what is permitted to enter into consciousness at any given moment, and does so by inhibiting most streams of information from intruding on a second-by-second basis. Inhibition is a very active process of repression. It is also very selective, in that the instant something is recognised as being of more current importance than something already in conscious thought, a switch of attention takes place. That is, the more important information is given priority over other streams of sensory data. Prioritisation of what merits attention is therefore another key element of the executive management function.

When ADHD is present, this process of inhibition and prioritisation does not function very well. There are times when it is visually very obvious to an individual that inhibition is underperforming. For example, when Tom was asked to remember a mixture of letters and numbers, he said he could 'see' them, but the background kept changing. He initially 'saw' them against a jungle-green background. This then took on a leaf texture before he was distracted by 'a bush encroaching on the numbers and letters'. Tatiana described how, when she closed her eyes, 'my brain takes a screen-saver mode with sounds and indescribable feelings as well. Although I am still, the shapes are moving around me as if I'm travelling so fast amongst and towards them.'

These sensory experiences appear to be a failure by the executive management systems to exert control – that is, suppress irrelevant information and maintain a reasonable level of activation. As there is also some evidence that synaesthesia occurs as a result of weaknesses in inhibition, it is not therefore that surprising to record a much higher frequency of synaesthesia in individuals with ADHD than in dyslexics and dyspraxics. This inhibition weakness could easily account for why those with ADHD are reported to be greater risk-takers than others (e.g. Brown, 2005), and this is reflected in a range of impulsive-type behaviours, such as saying something that is later regretted, taking drugs, sudden bursts of short-lived anger or frustration, or ill-advised sexual behaviour. There is some evidence that ADHD is, in some way, related to a right hemisphere disorder (e.g. Stefanatos & Wasserstein, 2006). As the right hemisphere is known to be dominant for visual and emotional processes, the heightened frequency of synaesthesia and emotional swings in individuals with ADHD may in part be a reflection of this hypothesised right hemisphere disorder.

Less obviously, ADHD is reflected in academic difficulties. For example, when confronted with having to sit down and write an essay, procrastination is very frequently reported. There are difficulties with staying focused on a task, and many with ADHD report they have so many ideas they find it difficult to be selective. It is my experience that even when writing just a short prose passage, the handwriting speed of those with ADHD is much slower than might be anticipated. Again this slowness reflects a difficulty with selecting what to write next from a palette of constantly changing ideas. As the handwriting speed of dyslexics is, in general, much faster than that of individuals with ADHD, slowness cannot therefore be attributed to a weak working memory, or a slow processing speed.

Understanding ADHD requires an appreciation of the complex nature of human thought processes, including their control mechanisms at both a neurological and cognitive level. For this reason many ADHD experts are uneasy with relying on the diagnostic criteria specified in the *Diagnosis and Statistical Manual of Mental Disorders* (DSM-IV) of the American Psychiatric Association. While the DSM-IV criteria capture some key aspects of ADHD, equally crucial experiences such as emotional instability are missing, and the criterion of signs of ADHD having to be present prior to the age of 7 is highly contentious. However, these reservations should not be used as reasons for not carrying out diagnostic assessments for ADHD, as there is convincing evidence that, in the UK at least, too many individuals with ADHD are still undiagnosed. For example, a survey of undergraduates (Pope et al., 2007) from four different universities revealed not only that over 10 per cent scored very highly on an ADHD checklist, but also their academic performance was below that of students with a lower ADHD score.

Unlike dyslexia or dyspraxia, ADHD has a neurological basis that, in many individuals, responds to medication. This neurological basis helps explain why, when under pressure or very interested in an activity, it is as if the brain self-medicates and hyper-focusing takes place. However, if the level of excitation drops following the meeting of a deadline or if there is a sudden loss of enthusiasm for an activity, the lack of inhibition of irrelevant thoughts again takes over. Given the number of people with undiagnosed ADHD – with all its possible consequences such as failure to achieve academic and career potential, bouts of emotional distress, a heightened risk of anti-social behaviour, whilst at the same time knowing there is an effective means of alleviating many, but not all, of these through medication – there are very good reasons for improving the diagnosis of ADHD and the provision of appropriate support.

Bibliography

Bourne, B. (2009) 'ADHD: Comorbity and communality'. Paper presented at the 9th International ADDIS Conference on Attention Deficit Hyperactivity Disorder, London, 30 March–1 April 2009.

Brown, T.E. (2005) *Attention Deficit Disorder: The Unfocused Mind in Children and Adults*, Yale University Press, CT.

Brown, T.E. (2009) 'ADHD & other disorders: A new view of comorbity'. Paper presented at the 9th International ADDIS Conference on Attention Deficit Hyperactivity Disorder, London, 30 March–1 April 2009.

Gillberg, C. & Kadesjö, B. (2003) 'Why bother about clumsiness? The implications of having developmental coordination disorder (DCD)', *Neural Plasticity*, 10, 59–68.

Hallowell, E.M. & Ratey, J.J. (1995) *Driven to Distraction: Recognising and Coping with Attention Deficit Disorder from Childhood through Adulthood*, Touchstone, NY.

Pope, D., Whiteley, H., Smith, C., Lever, R., Wakelin, H., Dudiak, H. & Dewart, H. (2007) 'Relationships between self-reported ADHD and dyslexia screening scores and academic performance in undergraduate university students: Implications for teaching, learning and assessment', *Psychology Learning and Teaching*, 6, 2, 114–120.

Stefanatos, G.A. & Wasserstein, J. (2006) 'Attention deficit/hyperactivity disorder as a right hemisphere syndrome', *Annals of the New York Academy of Sciences*, 931, 172–195.

Weiss, L. (1997) *A.D.D. and Creativity*, Taylor Trade Publishing, Lanham, MD.

Chapter 5

Visualisation and synaesthesia

It was late afternoon and the shadows were lengthening. Mary quickly hurried across the courtyard outside the British Museum, paused briefly to look up at the imposing pillars framing the main door, and stepped inside. She turned right and went into the King's Library. She has always wanted to see the Domesday Book. However, as soon as she entered the library the first book she saw on open display took her breath away. It was massive, and was open at a full-page painting of a bird of paradise. The yellow and red feathers appeared to glow with the light of the South Pacific.

As you were reading about Mary above, how did you experience what you were reading? Was it as if you heard the words being spoken in your head, or did you experience some or all of the paragraph visually – as a series of images or like a movie? If you are someone who visualises what you are reading, it may seem strange to ask these questions. However, in a study which asked students about their individual experiences when reading, at least a third said they did not experience any images (Grant, 2009). (Note. I am also someone who is a non-visualiser.) Of those who did experience a mental picture of what they were reading, the quality of visual imagery reported varied from poor to being in full colour and high definition, with about one third reporting good- or excellent-quality visualisation.

This degree of variation was not unexpected, for well over a hundred years ago, in 1880, Sir Francis Galton asked a range of individuals quite detailed questions about their ability to recall 'some definite object – suppose it is your breakfast table as you sat down this morning – and carefully consider the picture that rises before your mind's eye'. To his amazement he found that whereas most 'men of science' said 'mental imagery was unknown to them', many ordinary men and women 'declared they habitually saw mental imagery, and that it was perfectly distinct to them and full of colour'.

When I have asked individuals with a range of specific learning differences (dyslexia, dyspraxia and ADHD) to read the short passage above about Mary, the experiences they reported have varied greatly. Whereas some found it quite difficult to read and could remember very little of what they had just read, a few experienced what they were reading as if watching a movie playing in their mind. For example, Alex, who is dyslexic, described Mary as being aged 23–24, with long dark hair, and wearing a black dress that fell below her knees. As she entered the library there was 'a crown above the door'. He put the time of year as being 'late autumn'. Alex pointed out he has to 'see' what he is reading in order to understand the content and meaning.

Rob, who is both dyslexic and dyspraxic, described Mary as being in her mid-twenties, with black hair, and wearing a blue dress underneath a furry coat. He described the bird of paradise as being 'like a peacock, but red'. Anna, who is dyslexic, described Mary as being in her late twenties, with red hair and wearing a winter jacket. She described how, when reading, 'I put myself inside the text, I create a picture.' Kacey's experience (she has ADHD), was a little different for she 'was Mary' and she 'saw' the library as being 'similar to the last library' she visited.

The visual richness of these reading experiences is very important for a number of reasons. First, for people with a weak auditory working memory, being able to recall what they have read being played back as a series of images or like a movie is a very important memory aid. For example, Kacey was studying anatomy and she described how she could 'see' the muscles of the body but not remember their names. However, when given the name of a muscle, she was able to locate it. Second, it can be a source of creativity. Both Rob and Alex are film and TV students. When given a brief both are able to 'see' in their mind's eye how a finished film would look, even before they started shooting it. For example, Rob described how, when reading something that particularly interests him, 'it all flows out in front of me, like watching a film'. For this reason such individuals are often disappointed when they go to see a film based on a book they have read: 'It's not like I imagined it to be.'

There can also be a downside in that some books, particularly textbooks, are much more difficult to visualise than others, and these can then appear to be 'intimidating'. Also, because the personal visual images contain a great deal of information not present in the actual text, when tested on what they have read there is a good chance that irrelevant as well as relevant information will be recalled. For all four students, their visualisation was not confined to 'seeing' what they were reading but extended to music, words and numbers. For example, Rob described how, when listening to a song he likes, 'I create my own music video.' For Kacey, a particular piece of music triggers off a memory of where she was when she first heard it: 'I picture the event.' Anna, too, said some music brings back very vivid memories, but other pieces have a broader association, resulting in 'changes in shapes and colours'.

Anna's reference to 'shapes and colours' points towards the possibility that a very striking form of visualisation called synaesthesia may be present. Synaesthesia, like mental imagery, was a topic of considerable interest to psychologists before 1900 (Ward, 2008). Both topics then fell out of favour. However, after a lapse of over a hundred years, there has been a resurgence of research interest into these fascinating mental experiences. Synaesthesia is often described as being a blending of the senses. The most common blending is that of sounds with visual imagery. For example, when Rob was asked how he remembered a series of numbers that was read out, he said he could 'see' the individual numbers, with each being a different colour: 2 was light blue, 8 was purple, 3 was green, and 7 was yellow. When this exercise was repeated several hours later the colour he reported for each number was the same. As far as Rob was concerned this experience was just something that happens. However, this automatic 'seeing' of each number in a particular colour, and the consistency of this association over time, is a classic example of synaesthesia. Often the colour is very specific, e.g. blue is not just blue, nor even light or dark blue. It can be electric blue, teal, turquoise or 'the blue sky as reflected in a puddle'.

Another common sensory blending is that of letters of the alphabet and colours. For example, when a series of four letters was read out to Kacey, she said she not only 'saw' each letter immediately, but it had its own colour: *t* was green, *j* was grey, *a* was green and *x* was white. For some synaesthetes, some words can be both 'seen' and have different colours. When Cherry, who has ADHD, was asked to spell the name *Katherine*, she 'saw' it as being in a black font on a white background. However, when asked to spell *Katherine* with a C, as *Catherine*, it changed to red. The word *giraffe* was a mixture of yellow and blue, and the word *massage* was black on green. Dominic's letter–colour synaesthesia influences his emotional response to words. He gave as an example perceiving the words *their* and *there* as being aesthetically different, with *their* being ugly due to the last letter *r* being grey, whereas *e* is red (*th* is blue/green and *i* is turquoise.) Similarly he perceives the name *Catherine* as being 'nice', whereas *Katherine* is 'horrid'.

This ability to 'see' words was of considerable help to both Cherry and Dominic when they were learning to spell. Such an ability appears to be present from an early age. Lucy and Tracy are identical twins. Whereas Lucy 'sees' the word *giraffe* as being green and orange, her twin sister 'sees' *giraffe* as an 'orangey-red' word. Lucy said she and her sister used to argue when they were children as to whose colour was the right one. Different languages can take on different colours. Ellen described French as being 'light, pastel and green', while German 'is dark, grainer, still green but darker'.

There are occasions when words trigger an image, or images, specific to that word. Again, these images vary considerably in complexity and detail. The image is usually static, sometimes akin to a cartoon drawing or photograph. Less frequently it can be a moving image accompanied by sound. When Sara was given the word *giraffe* she described how she could 'see' a group of giraffes moving across the savannah, with the sun setting in the background. She could also 'hear' the chirping of cicadas. Sara spent hours as a child watching wildlife videos and it is as if, when given the name of an animal, it instantly triggers one of her childhood memories.

This type of episodic memory recall was very evident when Louise was given the word *giraffe*. She said it immediately evoked a memory of 'the first time I went to a zoo and saw a giraffe. I can even tell you what dress I was wearing.' On occasions the image can be so strong it results in a switch of concentration. For example, after I had finished giving a talk at a university, the president of the students' union – who has ADHD – came up to tell me that, when I asked the audience to describe any images automatically triggered by the word *giraffe*, 'my mind immediately went on a giraffe hunt and I didn't come back until the end of the lecture'. His tendency to be distracted by images is an everyday occurrence for a significant minority of individuals with ADHD, and this is explored later on in this chapter.

Occasionally I come across individuals who can only remember a word if it has an image. When the series of letters *t*, *m*, *j*, *x* was read out to Joe (a dyspraxic music student) he reported that *t* was yellow, *m* was blue, *x* was green and *j* was blue. When given the names of the days of the week they, too, were coloured, e.g. *Monday* was blue, *Tuesday* green, *Wednesday* red. However, he then pointed out that not only could he 'see' the word *Monday* in blue, but he also experienced images of rain and umbrellas 'flying in, flying out of view'. This richness accompanied other words as well.

When asked to name the capital city of Brazil, Joe described how he initially 'saw' a world map, followed by flashes of pictures emailed to him by friends who had visited Brazil, accompanied by snatches of music. A question about the Sistine Chapel immediately triggered a series of images of cherubs and angels and textures – 'with quite an earthy feel'. When someone is talking to him Joe not only 'sees' each word – a form of synaesthesia called ticker-tape synaesthesia – but each word is multi-layered with images. In addition, these images are often accompanied by sounds, emotions and textures he can feel. Consequently, Joe finds conversations quite exhausting, and has to take a break after about twenty minutes, particularly if the talk is fast paced.

The range of imagery that some individuals experience for words never ceases to amaze me. When I asked

Angelina, a dyspraxic Italian student, for her image of the word *epistemology*, she replied: 'I see myself inside a laboratory where knowledge is being generated and poured into a book.' As the word *epistemology* refers to the science of knowledge, her answer captured the meaning more richly than any dictionary definition of the word I have encountered. Angelina's synaesthesia is particularly complex. She described how she could not wear certain combinations of clothes because 'they don't taste right'. She also described different types of dog (e.g. spaniel and labrador) as having 'different tastes'.

Joe's and Angelina's synaesthesia is so rich and complex it interferes with some aspects of their everyday lives. For example, when Angelina reads a book or journal article, she has to stop after a short time because there is too much going on in her mind for her to take in what she is reading. I refer to this as sensory overload. Joe also experiences sensory overload, not only when taking part in a conversation but also when listening to a big band or orchestra. As he is a music student who specialises in singing, he prefers to perform with just one instrument or a small group. However, for many individuals visualisation, including synaesthesia, is a positive experience. Nisha, a dyslexic graphic design student, described how she experiences music as 'a moving, abstract image'. For this reason she listens to music when engaged in design work as it is a source of inspiration to her, and she has drawn upon this imagery when designing and printing T-shirts. Jamie is a dyslexic music technology student. He described how, when analysing the structure of a piece of music, he is aided by his music–colour–shape synaesthesia. For example, 'harsh percussion gives rise to red squares, the saxophone or flute creates soft, more fluid shapes . . . the bass is a blue colour'.

There are a number of examples of famous creative artists who draw deeply upon visualisation. David Lynch, film producer/director and photographer, described how the photographs he took to accompany the music of Danger Mouse 'are a representation of what went on in my head when I heard the music' (30 May 2009). When Tracey Emin, a famous British artist, was interviewed at the opening of her exhibition 'Those Who Suffer Love', she described how she is 'the custodian, the curator of the images that live in my mind' (25 May 2009). David Hockney, another famous British artist, is a music synaesthete. His set designs for operatic productions are influenced by the images he experiences when listening to the opera for which he has been commissioned to design.

There is no doubt that visualisation is a powerful way of thinking, in terms of understanding, remembering and problem-solving. However, although some authors (e.g. West, 1997; Davis, 1997) are convinced that a key defining characteristic, and therefore a strength, of being dyslexic is that visual thought is the primary mode of thought, the research evidence for this is weak. For example, Winner et al. (2000) found no clear link between dyslexia and visual–spatial skill. Regrettably, the vast majority of dyslexic research has focused on reading and spelling and not visualisation, or visual–spatial skills. There are therefore many questions that remain to be answered. The same is true for both dyspraxia and ADHD, where the situation may be much more complex. For example, Lovecky (2004) takes care to state that although many high functioning individuals with ADHD show a preference for visual–spatial learning, this is not true for all.

Throughout this book I have stressed the need to avoid sweeping generalisations about individuals with specific learning differences. This is particularly true when discussing visualisation, particularly as it takes many different forms and varies in vividness. For some time now I have been asking the individuals I see for assessment about their visualisation experiences when reading and when remembering numbers. I ask them to make a judgement about the quality of their imagery when reading, using a scale running from 1 (no or negligible imagery) to 5 (the images are in colour and high definition). I also read out a string of numbers and ask how they are remembered – by being mentally repeated or by being 'seen'.

On the scale of quality of visual imagery from 1 to 5, the average value for students with no specific learning differences was 2.6, with 36 per cent saying they experience no visualisation when reading. These figures are quite similar to those for dyspraxic students (average rating figure of 2.5, with 29 per cent reporting no visualisation when reading). However, both dyslexic and ADHD students reported a more vibrant visual experience when reading (average rating figures of 3.3 and 3.7 respectively), and a greater number experienced imagery when reading (only 18 per cent of dyslexics

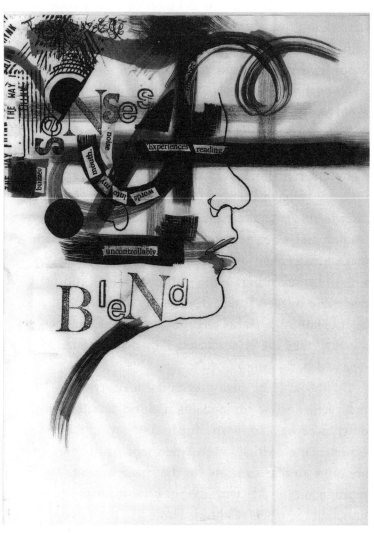

Illustration 5.1

and 12 per cent of those with ADHD reported no visualisation when reading). About half of dyslexics and dyspraxics reported they could 'see' numbers as they were read out, compared with just one in five of the general undergraduate population. The figure for individuals with ADHD was particularly high, with about three in four reporting 'seeing' numbers. (Note, in most cases numbers fade from view very quickly so only a minority can make use of their visualisation on tests of working memory.)

It must be stressed that these figures should only be taken as being indicative of trends. Nevertheless it appears reasonable to conclude that in general visualisation is more common in dyslexics and those with ADHD than in dyspraxics or those who have no specific learning difference. However, even amongst dyslexics and individuals with ADHD there is a significant range of experience of visualisation, from none to very strong. Even the type of visualisation varies.

I have come up with five categories to describe the type of mental imagery that individuals experience: episodic, paired-associate, creative, photographic or synaesthetic. The category 'episodic' refers to images that relate to an individual's personal memories, such as the place where a particular song was heard. 'Paired-associate' images have been learnt. For example, Kacey said the letter s was 'a green garter snake' – an image she remembered from when she was learning the alphabet, while for her the word *panda* triggered an image of a soft-drink can with a black and white panda logo. 'Creative' imagery occurs when an individual creates his or her own series of visual images or imaginary movie, for example when reading or listening to music. 'Photographic' imagery is very rare, but refers to the ability to recall in full detail something which has been seen previously, such as the page of a textbook. For example, Colin had such a memory. He described himself as being slower than other veterinary students when answering multiple-choice questions: 'I had to search for the page of the book that had the right information on it.' 'Synaesthetic' imagery refers to the sensory experience evoked by a very specific trigger such as a word, number or musical note or instrument. This system of categorisation is best thought of as being heuristic – an aid to thinking about types of mental imagery. The boundaries are not clear-cut and can and do merge into each other.

As part of my exploration of mental imagery I have looked at how frequently different groups of individuals report synaesthetic experiences. It is only in the past couple of years that a good, reliable figure for the general population has been reported. Simner et al.'s (2006) survey of a student population identified about one in 25 students as being synaesthetes. This figure is rather higher than most previous estimates. However, as most synaesthetes don't think there is anything unusual about their sensory experiences, it is not until very specific questions are asked that the rich and complex mental world of synaesthesia is glimpsed. Simner's figure of about one in 25 is in line with the incidence I have recorded for both dyslexics and dyspraxics. However, my initial survey (Grant, 2007) suggested this figure was much higher in individuals with ADHD. Since then I have seen many more people with ADHD, and about a third of these are synaesthetes. This is a strikingly high figure but tallies with my other data on the strong visualisation abilities of many with ADHD.

This figure, although very high, may not be too surprising, for one of the two main theories about how synaesthesia occurs is the disinhibited feedback theory (Grossenbacher & Lovelace, 2001). At its most basic, these two researchers suggest that the normal balance of excitation and inhibition that takes place between the vast number of nerve networks in the human brain is not always in balance at very specific points that vary from individual to individual. It is as if, when a message is being passed along a network, it excites other networks that might be related in some way to the original message. Usually anything that is not totally relevant will then be suppressed (inhibited). However, if this inhibition does not take place, both the original message and its non-inhibited partner message are experienced. This type of attentional difficulty has also been identified by other researchers as being crucial to understanding synaesthesia (e.g. Rich & Mattingly, 2002).

The concept of inhibition is very important, for one of the key characteristics of ADHD is a difficulty with maintaining ongoing control of conscious thought. That is, intrusive ideas and thoughts are distracting for they are not inhibited. It is therefore not at all surprising to record a much higher level of synaesthesia in those with ADHD than individuals with other specific learning

differences. The links between visual imagery, words
and attentional difficulties are revealed very clearly
when the mental world of individuals is explored. Many
individuals with ADHD, as well as a few dyslexics and
dyspraxics, describe themselves as experiencing two
parallel streams of consciousness simultaneously. The
following analogy captures this simultaneous experience.
You are in a room, listening to a discussion or play on
the radio. As you listen, a word or phrase triggers off an
image, or images, as if your attention has suddenly been
caught by a television in the other corner of the room
and you start watching it. You then realise you should
be attending to what is being said on the radio.
However, something else you hear triggers another image
and again you find yourself watching the television, but
this time it might well be a different channel. Sophie
described how, 'I see images when my mind wanders off
during a conversation. Sometimes I get so lost in my
world that when I return to this world I can't remember
what I was thinking about at all, but I know I've been
completely out of it and somewhere else.'

Sophie's difficulty with inhibiting the pull of visual
images while engaged in a conversation is reported by
many more individuals with ADHD than dyslexics or
dyspraxics. It is not the cause of ADHD. However,
Sophie's account of her attentional difficulties shows
that caution should be exercised in assuming that the
ability to visualise is always something to be welcomed.
For many individuals it adds a richness to everyday
thought that can only be guessed at by non-visualisers.
However, there are occasions when imagery is an

intrusion. Because each individual's sensory world is such a private one, we can only explore it by asking very specific questions. Fortunately, after a lapse of over a hundred years psychologists have rediscovered not only how fascinating visualisation is, but also how relevant it is to understanding an individual's everyday experiences.

Bibliography

Davis, R.D. (1997) *The Gift of Dyslexia*, 2nd edition, Souvenir Press, London.

Emin, T. (2009) Quoted in the *Guardian*, 25 May, G2, 17.

Galton, F. (1880) 'Statistics of mental imagery', *Mind*, 5, 301–318, http://psychclassics.yorku.ca/Galton/imagery.htm, accessed February 2009.

Grant, D.W. (2007) 'Incidence of synaesthesia and its diagnostic implications in adults referred for suspected specific learning difficulties during a 2-year period', *UK Synaesthesia Association Newsletter*, 3–4 November.

Grant, D.W. (2009) Unpublished, 'A survey of the reading and visualisation experiences of 86 students at Leeds Metropolitan University' (data collected by Daniel Grant, Sam Heathcote & Jane Kemshall).

Grossenbacher, P.G. & Lovelace, C.T. (2001) 'Mechanism of synesthesia: Cognitive and physiological constraints', *Trends in Cognitive Sciences*, 5, 1, 36–41.

Lovecky, D.V. (2004) *Different Minds: Gifted Children with AD/HD, Asperger Syndrome, and Other Learning Deficits*, Jessica Kingsley Publishers, London.

Lynch, D. (2009) Quoted in the *Los Angeles Times*, 30 May, D1.

Rich, A.N. & Mattingley, J.B. (2002) 'Anomalous perception in synaesthesia: A cognitive neuroscience perspective', *Nature Reviews: Neuroscience*, 3, 43–52.

Simner, J., Mulvenna, C., Sagiv, N., Tsakanikos, E., Witherby, S.A., Fraser, C., Scott, K. & Ward, J. (2006)

'Synaesthesia: The prevalence of atypical cross-modal experiences', *Perception*, 35, 1023 – 1033.

Ward, J. (2008) *The Frog Who Croaked Blue: Synaesthesia and the Mixing of the Senses*, Routledge, London.

West, T.G. (1997) *In the Mind's Eye: Visual Thinkers – Gifted People with Dyslexia and Other Learning Difficulties* Prometheus Books.

Winner, E., von Karolyi, C. & Malinsky, D. (2000) 'Dyslexia and visual–spatial talents: No clear link', *Boston College Perspectives*, Spring 1–8.

Further reading

Cytowic, R.E. & Eagleman, D.M. (2009) *Wednesday is Indigo Blue: Discovering the Brain of Synesthesia*, MIT Press, Cambridge, MA.

Chapter 6

Colours and reading

'It's just like a bra – it lifts and separates each word.'
Surprising as it may seem, an overlay of just the right
colour can change the visual appearance of a page of
text in unexpected ways. When Sonia placed the
coloured overlay that was the right colour for her over a
page of text she immediately noticed that she could see
the individual words much more clearly. Without the
overlay the words looked as is they were clumped
together, and she had to tease out each word from the
others around it when reading. Consequently she read
aloud in a hesitant manner. However, as soon as she
placed the overlay that best suited her over the text, the
words appeared to be separate from each other: 'The
words look like words.' Her reading speed improved and
she felt more relaxed and confident.

Sonia's experience is not unusual. Roughly 40 per
cent to 50 per cent of the dyslexics and dyspraxics I see
report a very noticeable and positive improvement in
the visual perception of text when using the coloured
overlay they find is best suited to them. Some individuals
with ADHD also report an improvement. For most, this
comes as a major surprise. Most people find it difficult to

describe what a page of words in a textbook or novel looks like to them before they try out a range of different coloured overlays. However, when they compare the appearance of a page of words with and without using the overlay that is the best colour for them, they are surprised by the difference. That is the point when they suddenly realise that words don't have to 'dance around on the page', clump together or 'pop up out of the page', and they don't have to be 'swamped by the glare of the white of the page'.

A number of dyslexics, dyspraxics and individuals with ADHD, without knowing it, experience visual stress when reading words printed in black on white paper. (This is why this book has been printed on slightly off-white paper.) The stress increases with decrease in the size of print. This may be one key reason why some people, who enjoyed reading when young, gradually stop reading for pleasure as they enter their teens. Children's books are generally printed in a large type face. However, as stories increase in complexity, print size decreases and an underlying visual stress factor then becomes more of an obstacle to the enjoyment of reading.

Visual stress also affects the reading of music. When this visual stress factor is present people often tire very quickly, whether reading words or music, and lose their place easily. Reading is not a pleasure – it has to be worked at – because the eyes are darting about. Eye movements are not smooth and controlled: 'It is as if the corner of my eye picks up a letter from somewhere on the page and flicks it into the word I'm reading.'

When this visual stress is present it can be overcome with the right coloured overlay, or the right coloured background when working at a computer monitor. The software ReadAble enables an individual to set the background colour on a computer monitor to the colour that suits them best. (This software is only available in the UK from iansyst: see Appendix.) There is no one colour that works for everyone. Usually the colour that is best for an individual is a very specific one. For some, lime-green is the most effective colour; for others, mint-green. For others, aqua works while blue doesn't.

It is only relatively recently that this positive impact of coloured overlays has been discovered. (Some say rediscovered.) Two people, working independently of each other, are credited with this discovery – Helen Irlen in California and Oliver Meares in New Zealand. That is why this visual stress syndrome is often referred to as the Meares–Irlen Syndrome. There are also alternative names, for example Helen Irlen (1991) named it Scotopic Sensitivity Syndrome. However, there is now a consensus, at least in the UK, to refer to it as visual stress.

Although the research of Irlen and Meares was highly controversial in the years immediately following the publication of their findings, most experts have since accepted that visual stress does exist, and that coloured overlays help to offset it. (Note. The most effective overlays have a slightly frosted appearance on one surface.) There is a major difference between demonstrating that coloured overlays offset visual stress and understanding the reason why they are effective. What is certain is that when visual stress is present it results in the poor coordination of eye movements. Second, we know that eye movements are controlled by the cerebellum (this is an area at the back of the brain that functions rather like an air traffic control centre). When reading, the eyes need to make very fast and very precise movements. They have to feed back information about the words to be read next as well as the word that is currently being read, so they have to scan forwards and backwards quite smoothly.

When visual stress is present, this smoothness is absent. Why this is so, and why colours help, is not fully understood. My interpretation is a simplistic one but captures the essence of what is probably happening. The cerebellum is linked to the retina (the light sensitive cells at the back of the eye) by two major pathways: the magnocellular pathway and the parvocellular pathway. The magnocellular pathway carries mainly black and white information, and works very fast. The parvocellular pathway mainly carries colour information from the retinal cells to the cerebellum and is slightly slower.

We know that, in some dyslexics, but not all, the magnocellular pathway is short of magno cells. This will then break up the smooth flow of information to the cerebellum. When this happens it is as if the cerebellum is trying to control the eyes in a fog. This results in an increase in mental energy being required, while eye movements become unfocused and dart about. However, when the right coloured overlay is found, information is redirected to the parvocellular pathway. Although this pathway is slower, the flow of information becomes smoother and more complete. It is as if the cerebellum now has a better picture because the fog has lifted and many more words can be seen. There is greater separation between the words and the lines of text – the 'bra' effect. Stress levels go down and speed of reading goes up.

If it was just a question of switching to the parvo pathway then any colour should help. As this is not the case another factor – colour pigment – has to be considered The back of our eyes contain a mixture of very specialised cells, some of which play a crucial role in helping with colour recognition. Some cells have a blue pigment, some a red one, and yet others have a green pigment.

Crucially, the proportion of the red and green pigments varies from person to person. We know that four different genes control the production of the red pigment, and another four genes control the production of the green pigment. Consequently, there are subtle differences in how individuals respond physiologically to the same colours. Hollingham (2004) summed it up very nicely: 'We all live in our own sensory world.'

This aspect of individuality is very important. While the available evidence suggests that everyone benefits to some extent from using a coloured overlay, for most people the improvement is very minor. However, for some people – particularly dyslexics and dyspraxics – the benefit is greater, for some much greater. It is important to stress that visual stress is sometimes observed in people who have no specific learning difficulties at all. I have also observed it in people who are colour-blind.

It is also independent of a sensitivity to light, a factor that affects some people.

Very occasionally, the impact of visual stress is so strong that an individual will feel nauseous and lose balance just by looking at a page of words. This was the case for Judith. Visual stress was present to such an extent that doctors wrongly diagnosed her as being epileptic and she had to give up work. Once she had been identified as being dyslexic with extreme visual stress and been provided with the coloured overlays that best suited her, she enrolled on a journalism course and began, in her mid-fifties, to successfully fulfil her life-long ambition. When visual stress is present in a moderate or severe form, the solution can quite literally be life-transforming. Coloured overlays, tinted spectacle lens or a computer screen adjusted to the most appropriate colour do not resolve most dyslexic or dyspraxic issues, but they can and do remove a significant barrier for a number of people.

Bibliography

Hollingham, R. (2004) 'In the realm of your senses', *New Scientist*, 31 January, 181, 40–42.

Irlen, H. (1991) *Reading by the Colors*, Avery Publishing Group, New York.

Chapter 7

Becoming creative

When asked whether being dyslexic had influenced his photography, the world famous photographer David Bailey replied: 'I feel dyslexia gave me a privilege. It pushed me into being totally visual.' (www.Showstudio.com, 12 February 2003).

There is a powerful public perception that being dyslexic means you are likely to be creative. For example, several years ago the website of the British Dyslexia Association had a long list of famous dyslexic people. Most of those named are well known for being creative, including Lord Richard Rogers (architect), Eddie Izzard (comedian), Lynda La Plante (script writer) and Benjamin Zephaniah (poet). Over 85 per cent of the famous names that were listed on the British Dyslexia Association website have made their mark in professions that we associate with being creative, such as the arts, design, music, writing and the media. There were virtually no scientists, engineers or business people in the list.

It has been known for a long time that the proportion of students who are dyslexic and are studying art or design is much higher than for other subjects such as business studies or the sciences. As success in art and design is related to being creative, does this imply that dyslexics are more creative than non-dyslexics? A number of people believe so.

Lord Laird, speaking in the House of Lords on 8 May 2000, claimed: 'Lateral thinking, problem solving, the ability to make creative leaps and see things from every angle are all skills associated with dyslexia.' The dyslexia.com website (28 July 2009) explains that dyslexia is a gift: 'Dyslexic people are visual, multi-dimensional thinkers. We are intuitive and highly creative . . . we think in pictures.'

I'm not so sure that dyslexics are born to be creative, visual thinkers. I suspect that it is the experience of *being* dyslexic that leads to many dyslexics becoming creative, and *being* dyslexic that influences their choice of which profession to enter. Surprising as it may seem, remarkably little research has examined the assumed link between being dyslexic and being creative. There is very extensive research on creativity. There is very extensive research on dyslexia. However, very little research has been carried out that looks at both dyslexia and creativity together. I suspect it is the lack of research that has allowed the myth to develop that being dyslexic means you must be a creative visual thinker as well.

It is worth reading David Bailey's comment again. 'I feel dyslexia gave me a privilege. It pushed me into being totally visual.' Note his use of the word 'pushed'. It is intuitively easy to understand how an association between dyslexia, art and creativity has arisen. If you experience problems with reading, spelling and maths, and with expressing your ideas in writing, success in many subjects becomes difficult to achieve, no matter how hard you try. Subjects such as art, design and technology, which are more practical and require less reading and writing than most other subjects, therefore become attractive. Consequently, when dyslexic school pupils get a chance to choose which subjects they want to study, they tend to opt for these subjects. Art and design are also perceived as being the more creative subjects. The choice made at school then tends to restrict the subjects that can be studied at undergraduate level, which in turn influences career options.

This is what I call the 'least barriers' route. The same thing happens in the sciences and engineering as well. Many dyslexic and dyspraxic science and engineering students tell me they particularly enjoy the practical aspects of these subjects, and that they find writing reports much easier than writing essays because reports have a clear structure. Many dyslexic and dyspraxic students therefore decide to specialise in science or engineering because there are fewer barriers to success than if they were to choose humanities or social science subjects.

It is important to note that as science and engineering require good mathematical skills this excludes a number of dyslexic and dyspraxic students. Whereas some find maths easy, others find maths very difficult. As the arts and most design areas do not require mathematical skills, the least barriers principle will again apply, and some students will find themselves being pushed towards these subjects.

Although I have met a number of students who would automatically have chosen art, design or the sciences irrespective of whether they were dyslexic or not, I have also met students who have felt pushed towards these subjects because they presented fewer barriers to success. This push towards art and design is much more powerful for someone who is dyslexic than for someone who is dyspraxic or has ADHD.

In the case of a person with dyspraxia or ADHD, reading and spelling levels are in harmony with the level of verbal reasoning, so subjects such as English and history don't appear intimidating. In addition, the typical dyspraxic features of a poor sense of three-dimensional visualisation and weak fine hand–eye coordination will affect skills of drawing and painting. These two factors are likely to discourage someone who is dyspraxic from specialising in art or design, while the need to spend weeks working on an art project is a discouraging feature for some with ADHD.

When I first began carrying out dyslexia diagnoses for students studying art or design I expected to find these students would have a level of visual reasoning that was at least as good as their verbal reasoning, if not better. In practice, the opposite is often the case. I have been surprised by how many art and design students have scored higher on Verbal Comprehension than on Perceptual Organisation. I had not expected this at the time, but it may be surprisingly easy to explain.

I suspect there are two key factors at play here. First, there is the least barriers factor. That is, as described above, some students go on to study art and design, not because there are naturally inclined to these subjects, but because they sense they will do better in them than subjects that require good reading and writing skills. Second, the study of art and design has changed considerably over the past decade to now embrace a range of new skills as well as the more traditional ones.

For example, installation art has become a medium that a number of students now choose to specialise in. Installation art draws on non-traditional art skills such as sound design and video production. Consequently, a dyslexic art student who thinks verbally rather than visually can be successful on a fine art degree by electing to work with installations. The same applies to students of broadcasting. Just like art and design, broadcasting encompasses a wide range of specialisms. Some aspects of broadcasting, such as camera operation, lighting and set design, are very visual. Other aspects, such as script-writing and presenting, are strongly verbal. Being stronger at verbal than visual reasoning is not the obstacle to success in art it would have been some years ago.

So far we have discussed the push factor as one reason why there are likely to be more dyslexic students taking art and design than other subjects. To succeed as an artist or designer you also need to be creative. It is said by a number of people that being creative is a dyslexic strength. I feel this might be the case for some dyslexics – but not all – although not for the reason usually given.

Before explaining this further, it is useful to look at what makes for successful creativity. Most researchers agree on two key aspects. First, creativity is about

finding original solutions that are effective. The key
point about this definition is that there is equal
emphasis on both originality and effectiveness. Novelty
or newness for its own sake doesn't count. The solution
must also work.

Second, being creative is a basic human trait.
Without an ability to be creative we would be robotic
and unable to undertake such basic activities as speaking
and thinking. Being creative is not reserved for those we
call geniuses. Being creative is what we all do every day.
That does not mean, however, that we all have the
same level of creativity. Some people are more creative
than others.

There are several reasons for this. Although it would
be wrong to discount natural differences in creative
ability between people, it is possible to learn techniques
to become more creative. We can also work harder at
achieving creative solutions. This aspect of working
harder may seem a little unusual, but in fact research
has shown that it is often the critical factor as to why
some people succeed to a greater extent than others.

Arriving at an effective creative solution is not just a
matter of waking up one day and knowing the answer to
a question. This stage in the problem-solving process is
known as illumination. To reach this point requires two
previous stages: preparation and incubation. Preparation
is about identifying what the question should be as well
as researching possible avenues to explore and gathering
relevant information. Incubation describes the process of
leaving a question ticking over in the back of your
mind, and it follows on from the preparation stage.

The stage of preparation is influenced enormously by the amount of hard work that is put into this stage. When the life history of creative achievers is examined, this factor stands out. For example, when the painter Turner was asked for advice about painting, he replied: 'The only secret I have is damned hard work.'

The researcher Ochse captures this aspect of hard work perfectly in her quote, 'before the Gates of Excellence the High Gods have placed sweat – the sweat of labour – often mingled with the sweat of pain' (1990, page 132). If there is one unifying factor running through the accounts of people who are creatively successful, it is this capacity for hard work.

Most dyslexic and dyspraxic students I have seen mention how much more effort they have to put into their homework and university work to just get the same grade as their fellow non-dyslexic and non-dyspraxic students. Because they know it takes them longer than others to research and write essays, they start work much earlier than others, and all aspects of the process take longer, perhaps three or four times as long. It is therefore highly likely that this sets up a persistent work habit that is particularly beneficial in creative endeavours.

We can see this commitment to hard work in the comment by Peter, a dyslexic ceramics student, who told me: 'My attitude is, because of who I am, I got into a habit of working much harder and thought, if I was going to compete, my efforts would have to be higher and that doesn't stop –whatever I do, whether it's written, physical or creative.'

There are other key factors that might be at work as well. Studies of the life histories of creative achievers (Ochse, 1990) reveal that many saw themselves as being different from other children, and they often received considerable encouragement from their parents. I have been struck by the number of dyslexic and dyspraxic students who have voiced their feelings of being different from other children. Emma's statement captures the childhood experiences of a number of dyslexic and dyspraxic students I have met: 'I was certainly different, certainly – I remember feeling different . . . I used to spend a lot of time on my own and I did things on my own . . . I used to go home and cry.' Very often these students have enjoyed the support of at least one parent who has realised that they are struggling and has tried to be as supportive as possible. When Emma talked about her parents she said: 'He always encouraged me, my mum always encouraged me, she always read to me . . .'.

If we put these three factors together, the need to work harder than others, feelings of being different, and supportive parents, we can see that the formative years for a dyslexic or dyspraxic child help to shape a way of thinking and behaving that fosters being creative. In other words, it is the experience of being dyslexic or dyspraxic that is important for becoming creative, not the dyslexia or dyspraxia itself.

Having said that it is the experience of being dyslexic or dyspraxic that is important, other possible contributory factors to being a creative thinker should not be totally discounted. For example, brainstorming is a technique that many students are taught to help them generate ideas. This technique is often used as a starting point when a brief is given out. It has previously been suggested that a limited working memory capacity results in ideas slipping in and out of conscious thought in an almost random manner. This results in a transient and chaotic experience – almost like an ongoing brainstorming session.

As a weak working memory often results in people going off at tangents, more unusual associations of ideas tend to be formed. Emma, a fashion student, was well aware of just how quickly her mind jumps around: 'Everything around you is inspiring, music from passing cars, faces at bus stops.' This type of 'brainstorming' experience, which results from the limited capacity of conscious auditory memory, is therefore more likely to throw up more unusual combinations of ideas, with the consequence that unplanned solutions have more chance of occurring.

This may be a significant factor in helping someone to arrive at a new way of thinking about a question. Although this may help at the initial stage of problem-solving, it can sometimes be a distraction. Some students find it very difficult to stay focused on their main idea as they work towards the end product, because they keep going off at tangents. Peter, a ceramics student, was familiar with this experience: 'There are so many ideas you have to be selective. Once I cast a vessel I have a thousand ideas from it.' Peter knew that one of his strengths, the ability to generate lots of ideas, could also become a liability unless he kept it under control.

Because some dyslexic students find they can be sidetracked easily, they prefer to select subjects with an inbuilt structure. Sarah, a composer and drummer, spent a year on a photography degree course before changing to a degree in popular performance music. Because composing has a clear structure to it (you lay down the drums and bass parts before adding the parts for guitar, keyboards and lyrics), she felt much more at ease. She told me that 'structure has always been quite important – I find structure helped me quite a bit and I find without it I'm sometimes a bit lost – I need to do a lot more work without it.'

The limited capacity of auditory working memory may also force a reliance on other sensory memories, such as visual, tactile and kinaesthetic ones. We can see this factor at work in Sarah's comment: 'I can hear the sounds and maybe hear it in the vocals as well, but also when I'm hearing rhythm in songs I'm always imaging it physically and visually as well – that can help me remember.' Sarah's use of imaging rhythm physically and visually is partly driven by the ease with which she forgets things: 'I had a really great idea, it's gone – it's the best idea I've had and it's gone . . . it's like grrrr . . . when I don't write things down and it's a good idea and it's gone, it's frustrating.'

For many students, a better technique than just writing ideas down when trying to organise them is to map ideas visually. For example, I remember showing a student how the mind-mapping software Inspiration can be used to capture ideas in a visual form. After using it for a couple of minutes he said, 'That's the way I think.'

Because of his very limited working memory he found he needed to capture and organise his ideas visually. That way, he could see all his ideas together. For some dyslexics and dyspraxics who have become proficient at visual thinking, this becomes their preferred way of thinking. I emphasise the word 'some', for not all dyslexics and dyspraxics are visual thinkers, but are much more comfortable thinking verbally, even with its limitations.

A weak working memory may also contribute in quite an unusual way to creative thinking. The chapter on sleep (Chapter 10) reports that many dyslexic, dyspraxic and ADHD students have difficulty getting to sleep. During this time many find themselves going over and over things that happened during the day and things they need to do. Consequently, this often involves thinking about a brief they have been given. For some students this can be their most creative thinking time.

Being creative frequently involves bringing together very different sets of information. Whereas this can be difficult in the daytime because of other competing demands for attention, the stillness of night ensures there is a greater chance of the necessary elements coming together. Because getting to sleep, for some, can take so long, there is an even greater chance of an appropriate solution being arrived at. This can be viewed as an enforced opportunity to work harder than the non-dyslexic or non-dyspraxic person. However, there is little point in arriving at the perfect solution only to forget it by morning. This is the reason why some students have a 'night book'. If they have a good idea while trying to get to sleep they immediately write it down. They can then relax knowing they have 'captured' their idea.

The additional time for creative thinking at night may be important in that, for some dyslexics and most dyspraxics, speed of visual processing is often a weak point. This factor affects speed of learning. Creative thinking is a stage process. The beginning stage, preparation, requires research which usually involves the acquisition of new facts, ideas, techniques, even questions to ask. This takes time.

A slow speed of visual processing, allied with a weak working memory, slows down the rate at which someone who is dyslexic or dyspraxic can learn. So reaching the point at which a creative solution can occur may be a slower process than for a non-dyslexic or non-dyspraxic student. It is important to note that, even if all the preparatory work has been undertaken, not everyone will arrive at an effective creative solution at the same time. Such slowness often results in many dyslexics and dyspraxics knowing that they are capable of high-quality work, but needing to proceed at their own pace. This is reflected in their dislike of having to work under pressure.

The factor of slowness of processing speed is an important one for some art and design students, as in some instances it will be reflected in drawing style. Many art and design courses still require drawing skills. Some people can draw rapidly and fluidly, putting down confident lines, but not everyone can do this. In the case of someone who has a high level of visual thinking, but a slow speed of visual processing, it's as if their brain is thinking faster than their hand can execute an idea. This can then be reflected in a style of drawing that consists of smaller strokes, lines that overlap, and fainter marks. This style of drawing may look scratchy or hairy. For example, Hannah described her drawing style as being scratchy.

Some courses, such as fashion, place an emphasis on fast sketching (for example, when making sketches of models on catwalks and creating roughs). Tanya is a very gifted fashion student. However, when given a brief and asked to produce a number of roughs, she was unable to work at the same speed as other students. Whereas her fellow students could produce about twelve rough sketches of their initial ideas in an hour, Tanya was able to produce only about four. In addition to sketching slowly, she described her sketches as having a wooden feel to them, as she lacked fluency. Yet by the time she had completed a design brief, her finished garments were first class.

Tanya, Hannah, Emma, Peter and Sarah are typical of many dyslexic students. They are talented, hard working and quite individual. As the quotes above illustrate, they think and work in different ways. This individuality is important for it reveals that the process of being creative takes different forms. This makes generalisation difficult. Just as there are various types of dyslexia there are different creative processes. Arguably the common feature is the relationship between being successful and hard work.

It is also important to note that the arts and design are not the sole provinces of creativity. All aspects of

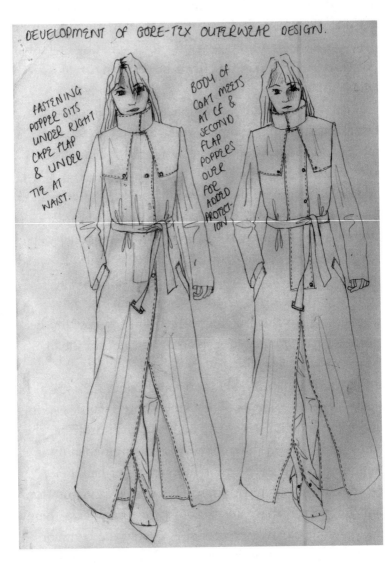

Illustration 7.1

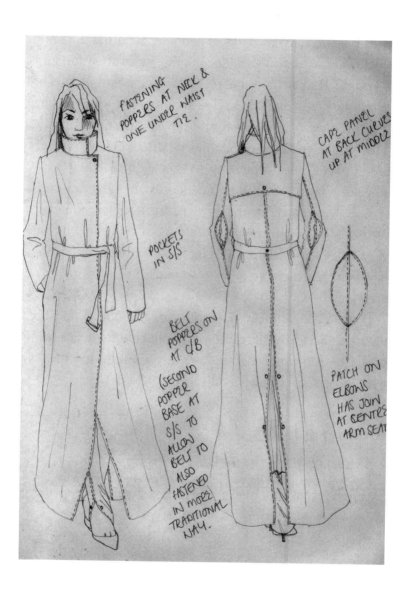

FASTENING
POPPERS AT NECK &
ONE UNDER WAIST
TIE.

POCKETS
IN S/S

BELT
POPPERS ON
AT C/B

(SECOND
POPPER
BASE AT
S/S TO
ALLOW
BELT TO
ALSO
FASTENED
IN MORE
TRADITIONAL
WAY.

CAPE PANEL
AT BACK CURVES
UP AT MIDDLE

PATCH ON
ELBOWS
HAS JOIN
AT CENTRE
ARM SEAT

employment require people who are creative. Although relatively few people will have heard of Guy Hands, he is a dyslexic City of London financier who has a worldwide reputation for developing innovative funding methods. Rather more people will have heard of Richard Branson. He is dyslexic and is renowned worldwide for spotting new opportunities and developing new services. The Virgin group of companies differs radically from most others. It is interesting to speculate whether the eclectic Virgin group of companies might be a reflection of a dyslexic mode of thought. Anita Roddick, founder of the Body Shop, was another famous dyslexic who was very successful in business. Her dyslexic daughter, Sam Roddick, has more recently also made her mark by creating the Coco de Mer chain of shops.

Being dyslexic means experiencing childhood and the teenage years in a different way from non-dyslexics. It would be surprising if this was not then reflected in what a person becomes and elects to do.

Bibliography

Ochse, R. (1990) *Before the Gates of Excellence: The Determinants of Creative Genius*, Cambridge University Press, Cambridge.

Chapter 8

Sports, genes and evolution

Dyslexia is at least as old as humankind. This may appear to be an amazing claim to make but this chapter goes from known facts to 'thinking outside the box'. This chapter explores some questions that are overlooked or ignored in almost every book on dyslexia. The first of these questions asks why dyslexia is so widespread.

Does dyslexia have an ancient evolutionary history?

I live and work in London where the mixture of cultures and races is extremely diverse. Consequently, I see students from many different countries. To give you some idea of this diversity, I have carried out diagnostic assessments for students from China, Fiji, Iceland, India, Iran, Israel, Kuwait, Malaysia, Nigeria, Russia and Uganda. In spite of very different languages and writing scripts, there are very striking and uniting factors. Each student experienced significant difficulties with learning to read and spell at school. Every student has always had problems with memory in spite of good verbal reasoning skills, and they are all slow at processing visual information. This universality of typical dyslexic characteristics did not come as a surprise to me, for I was quite familiar with pioneering cross-cultural research into reading difficulties carried out by Stevenson et al. in 1982.

Stevenson et al. carried out their research in three countries – America, Japan and Taiwan. In each country they assessed the performance of a representative, general sample of 10-year-old schoolchildren by measuring reading ability as well as verbal and visual reasoning skills. In each country they identified children who had reading skills below expectation. The percentage of children with unexpected reading difficulties in all three countries was approximately the same – around 6 per cent. This research was very important because it demolished the myth that dyslexia is not found in children taught to read and write in Japanese or Chinese. That is, in spite of very different writing scripts, approximately the same number of American, Japanese and Chinese children experience unexpected difficulties with learning to read. This research also demonstrated that in cultures where there is no word for dyslexia, dyslexic children are considered to be responsible for the difficulties they experience because they are not working hard enough. In societies that have no word for dyslexia, and attribute problems at school to not working hard enough, dyslexic students find it very hard to explain to their parents what being dyslexic means.

What are the implications of dyslexia being found in all national groups? Imagine walking into a room that contains six dyslexic students, each from a different country – there is a Chinese student and the others are from Kuwait, Kenya, the West Indies, Sweden and Pakistan. The obvious racial differences would be immediately striking but there would be no way of knowing any of them were dyslexic unless they mentioned it or you had been informed beforehand. However, in spite of such obvious physical differences, their neuropsychological profile would be the same. To observe such a similarity in spite of very different physical racial characteristics can mean only one thing in evolutionary terms: being dyslexic predates the point at which racial differences began to evolve. In evolutionary terms dyslexia appears to have been present since the beginning of humankind.

The only other interpretation is to argue that there is an environmental factor common to all cultures that triggers the development of dyslexia. For example, could diet be such a factor? I'm not convinced that this line of argument stands up to close scrutiny as a good general explanation of why dyslexia occurs. For example, the diet of a student born in the UK, but whose parents are from Afghanistan or Iceland, might be different from the diet of their grandparents. However, if you then discover that one of their grandfathers or grandmothers is suspected of being dyslexic, it is highly likely that their grandparent's diet was very traditional. In other words, in spite of changes in diet across generations, dyslexia is a constant.

When considering the proposal that diet is an important factor in helping to explain why dyslexia occurs, it is important to stress that there is a big difference between rejecting diet as a *good general explanation* and allowing for some exceptions. The question of diet is currently important in that some researchers have argued that our current intake of an important fatty acid, Omega-3, which is vital to brain function, is much lower than it was several centuries ago. However, this line of argument overlooks the fact that dyslexia is present in both Japan and Iceland, two countries with a high consumption of fish, a very important source of Omega-3. The inescapable facts are that dyslexia is widespread and the incidence appears to be roughly the same across countries. What is more, it is known to be hereditary.

As a generalisation, if you are dyslexic there is a one in two chance that each child you have will also be dyslexic. As you will know by now, dyslexia is quite a complex condition. Because of this complexity, and because the inheritance factor is not a straightforward one, most geneticists (e.g. Fisher and DeFries, 2002) are in agreement that dyslexia is an expression of a combination of genes rather than there being a single dyslexic gene. (It is in fact very unusual to find a one gene, one condition association. What strikes most geneticists is how complex things are, not how simple. For example, eye colour is determined by upwards of nine genes.)

Recently, geneticists have discovered a new level of complexity. Genes can be switched on and off by what are known as histones. Histones are a special kind of chemical messenger influencing how hard genes have to work at creating proteins – from not working at all to going into overdrive. The new level of complexity means that three people can have the same gene, but for one person that gene may be switched on and working at just the right level, for another the gene might be working but only slowly, while in the third person the gene may be switched off. In theory, this means that what you eat, drink or take in from your environment could in some way potentially influence histone production. So it is just possible that diet may be a factor. If it is, it is likely to influence the action of a couple of genes at the most, not the complicated combination of genes that underlie being dyslexic. However, in spite of the claims that have been made for the importance of diet, claims that are frequently controversial, to date there is no sound research evidence that I am aware of that dyslexia can be 'cured' by changes of diet.

Because of this genetic and histone complexity, making predictions about whether a child with a dyslexic parent might be dyslexic is fraught with difficulties (and dyslexic gene screening is a long way off). Current prediction is based on probabilities, which means that while it is highly likely that some children with a dyslexic parent will be dyslexic, not all children will be. Because of the complex nature of dyslexia, the severity and type of dyslexia will also vary within a family.

As dyslexia is known to run in families this enables an intriguing question to be addressed. Would it be possible to be dyslexic in a preliterate society? Education for all children within a given society is a very recent

development. Only about 150 years ago education was
for the privileged few, even within almost any of today's
developed nations. So, could one of your ancestors have
been dyslexic 150 years ago if they had not been taught
to read and write? For example, if you are dyslexic,
and your mother or father is dyslexic, could you then
discover that your great-great-great-grandfather or
mother was also dyslexic even though they never went
to school? (150 years is only about six generations.)

The answer depends entirely on how dyslexia is
defined. If the only criterion is that verbal reasoning
abilities are significantly higher than reading and
spelling skills in spite of adequate education, then
dyslexia cannot exist in someone who has not formally
been exposed to the teaching of reading and writing.
This definition does, however, then give rise to a
developmental problem – dyslexia cannot exist in
pre-school children either. How then can someone be
diagnosed as being severely dyslexic at the age of
8 or 9, but be said not to be dyslexic when they are
about 3 or 4?

If a broader definition of dyslexia is used, then a child
can be dyslexic at the age of 6 months as well as the
age of 3 years, or 8 or 15. Broader definitions include
unexpected difficulties with reading and spelling as being
just one facet of being dyslexic. Other aspects include
memory and concentration weaknesses, and a slow speed
of visual processing, and these would be expected to be
present from birth. In principle, it should therefore be
possible it diagnose someone as being dyslexic or
dyspraxic soon after they are born.

Because some of the key neuropsychological features of dyslexia are shared with dyspraxia and ADHD, care should be taken when carrying out a diagnosis on a young child to distinguish dyslexia from dyspraxia and ADHD. Just as an infant can therefore be said to be dyslexic before starting school, so also can it be stated that dyslexia existed in preliterate societies. This is not such a radical proposal as it may seem. Andrew Ellis (1985) voiced the opinion that whatever dyslexia might eventually turn out to be, it would almost certainly be found to have little to do with reading or spelling.

Why distractibility might be a survival advantage

The ability to remember and to forget is fundamental to human survival. Without being able to remember, everything would be a new sensation. Without an ability to forget we would be swamped with information. The ability to remember and forget is a basic survival process for animals as well. In evolutionary terms, the ability to remember and forget must have evolved at a very early stage in the development of animal life. In spite of this, these processes are still little understood, other than being known to be very complex. Such complexity is a strong indication that they must be genetically complex as well.

As with the inheritance of any process that is known to be complex, significant variation is to be anticipated. This is in fact the case. I have encountered students with photographic memories; I have met a student who has difficulty recognising the face of her own child; I have come across students whose working memory is so weak that remembering three consecutive numbers is almost impossible; others can recall virtually nothing of their childhood. Significant variation between all types of memory, whether that be visual memory, working memory or long-term memory, is a feature of human life.

Because a very poor memory can be disruptive of everyday life, it would be anticipated that evolutionary pressures would favour the survival of those with the best memories. This pressure would have been exerted over many millennia, for a tendency to forget what you have just set out to do, to daydream more than others, or having a difficulty with organisation or learning quickly, would arguably be a disadvantage in almost any society, whether nowadays or 100,00 years ago.

If evolutionary pressures favour the survival of those with an effective memory, then why is a weak working memory such a prominent feature of many dyslexics? To answer this question requires speculation and, in order to address it, I will explore the evolutionary line of thought a little further. I will then take what may appear to be, at first sight, a very unusual approach by talking about the relationship between sports and dyslexia and dyspraxia.

There is no doubt that a weak working memory is a source of frustration for many dyslexics, dyspraxics and individuals with ADHD. It is, however, just possible that long ago in our evolutionary past a weak working memory might actually have been an advantage rather than a disadvantage. This advantage might have come about because there is a strong tendency for people with a weak working memory to be easily distracted.

Many dyslexics, dyspraxics and individuals with ADHD often describe themselves as easily losing concentration. In general, the greater the working memory deficit the more easily distracted someone will be. This is a major disadvantage if you are working in a library, an office or studio, or at home, and every time you hear a noise or sense a movement you look up from what you are doing. Such ease of distractibility would, however, have been a major advantage half a million or more years ago, for our brains evolved to enable us to survive in an uncertain and dangerous world.

A constant fear of our ancestors would have been ending up as lunch for a hungry animal. Under such circumstances, being extremely alert and very sensitive to sudden movement or unexpected noises would have been an important survival mechanism. This kind of behaviour is evident when you watch a bird or squirrel feeding. It may well have been the case that those individuals who were the most easily distracted were those who had the greatest chance of escaping being eaten.

However, as our ancestors evolved, social rules and language would also have emerged and became more complicated. These changes could only have come about if they had also been accompanied by increases in working memory, for it is working memory that is the hub of our sense of consciousness and deliberation. Evolutionary pressures would therefore have then favoured the development of memory processes, particularly working memory. But this pressure would have been pulling against the much older pressure of distractibility being an advantage.

Although the association between ease of distractibility and survival would have been a very powerful survival mechanism some millennia ago, I don't think it has entirely disappeared. Those individuals who are best suited to an environment are those most likely to survive and pass on their genes. Sensitivity to the unexpected would be an important characteristic. So would physical prowess. This takes me to the next stage of my thinking outside the box.

Why are dyslexics good at sport?

Over the past nine years I have assessed many students who have achieved a very high level of sporting achievement. These students include a world sailing champion, a European champion in taekwondo, a UK cycling time trial national champion, a UK national cross-country runner, a Malaysian national swimming champion, a Chilean bronze medallist in gymnastics and a Swedish bronze medallist in free-style skating. To date I have diagnosed as being dyslexic twenty-one individuals who have achieved a national or international level of sporting success, and about one hundred who have represented their county.

For some years now I have asked all the people I see questions about their attitude to sport and sporting ability when building up a personal history profile. I do this because it helps to distinguish dyspraxics from dyslexics. As a rough generalisation you would anticipate that dyslexics would enjoy sport at school because it provides an escape from subjects involving reading and writing. On the other hand it would be expected that dyspraxics would dislike sports because of the need for good coordination skills. As ever with the understanding of dyslexia and dyspraxia, the reality is more complicated. Some dyslexics hate sports. A few dyspraxics are enthusiastic about sports and reach a high level.

Of the six dyspraxic students I have met who have achieved at a national level in sporting performance, two had rowed for their country (one for England and one for Italy). However, five of the six were also dyslexic. This once again raises an intriguing question about the relationship between sports and dyslexia. I have also encountered dyspraxics who, in spite of being very poor at sports, have still enjoyed sports. In a number of instances ADHD has also been present. In this case it is as if by taking an active part in sports excess energy can be run off. This was very clear in William's case. During his two years at college his marks changed from very good in his first year to being poor in his second year. He explained that during his first year he had cycled every evening. However, following the loss of his bike in his second year he had not been able to go cycling. Consequently he found it very difficult to sit down to his college work in the evening.

Aisha is also a very restless person. Like William, she is a dyspraxic individual with ADHD. In spite of not being fast at running, or good at catching, she 'loved team sports'. She described herself as becoming 'lonely and bored' in solo sports, with the consequence her level of motivation dropped rapidly. Like many individuals with ADHD, she would take up a new sport with considerable enthusiasm, only for her enthusiasm to decrease markedly, when she would then embark on another sport. Consequently she had engaged in many team sports, but without staying with one long enough to become proficient at it. In her mid-teens she took up dancing with enthusiam. Althought her dance skills were poor, Aisha described meeting lots of different peolple when she went dancing as being a powerful motivator.

It is very important to keep in mind that enthusiasm for sports is not the same as being good at sport. Enthusiasm is, however, very important because of its motivational aspect. Being dyslexic or being dyspraxic or an individual with ADHD brings with it certain challenges. For example, a weak working memory results in difficulties with those sports that require multi-tasking. As an example, consider all the different elements that have to be thought about when learning to play netball. These include remembering which area of the pitch to stay within – move outside this and you give away a penalty. You also have to think about ball control, which way you are playing and where your team mates are. You also have to take note of what they are saying or indicating. Because you have to take account of so many things simultaneously you need to be able to multi-task to be a good player, especially when learning the game. It is not surprising that dyslexics and dyspraxics and individuals with ADHD say they tend to give away more penalties than others when learning to play a team sport.

In general, team sports such as netball require more in the way of multitasking than individual sports such as running or swimming, for the rules are often complex and there is a need to pay close attention to what your team members as well as the opposition are doing. For example, I have met rugby players who have reached a high level but have always frustrated their coach and team members because they cannot remember the line-out calls. (These are usually in code so that the opposition cannot work out who the ball will be thrown to.) One rugby player described how the team captain would stand behind him in the line out and tell him when to jump as he could never remember the line-out codes.

An analysis of the data I have collected from the dyslexic and dyspraxic students I have seen reveals that they are more likely to choose, and then succeed at a high level in individual sports such as swimming and track athletics, than in team sports such as football, netball and basketball. It is therefore not surprising that the students I have seen who have reached a national or higher level of success, twenty of the twenty-one participate in individual sports. It is also not unexpected that Hannah's illustration reveals her sport to be judo, another individual sport.

Hannah's illustration reveals that, like many dyslexic and dyspraxic students who enjoy sport, she has to work harder at succeeding (see Illustration 8.1). Even when a dyslexic or dyspraxic prefers to play in a team sport, I have noticed a tendency for them to play in defence.

Illustration 8.1

If you think back to a typical neuropsychological profile for dyslexics and dyspraxics, visual reasoning skills are generally better than speed of visual processing. That is, there is a good ability to read the game but a lack of the swiftness of response that is the hallmark of a striker. However, once again it is wise to avoid applying a generalisation to all dyslexics or dyspraxics. Sir Jackie Stewart is dyslexic. He is also a world grand prix motor car racing champion. An exception to a preference for individual sports has to be made for individuals with ADHD. My experience is that of those who enjoyed taking part in sports at school they preferred team sports. This is not a surprise as team sports are both more social and unpredictable on a moment-to-moment basis, factors that are important in maintaining a high level of concentration.

Not all dyslexics and dyspraxics enjoy sport. For some, particularly dyspraxics rather than dyslexics, early attempts at taking part in sport and PE at school are so humiliating that they eventually give up and often seek to avoid having to take part in PE or games at school. The humiliation of being the last to be picked for a team especially when you are desperate to play, the bullying that is often experienced by those who are poor at sports, all serve to erode self-confidence and self-esteem. Of those dyslexic students who enjoy taking part in a sport, a surprisingly high proportion go on to be really good at it. Approximately one in eight of the dyslexic students I have assessed have excelled at some aspect of sport (Grant, 2008). I have used as a measure of excellence whether a student has been chosen to represent their county at one or more sports and used equivalent measures for overseas students (e.g. representing a province in France, Land in Germany or state in the USA or Australia). To be selected to represent a county or equivalent in a chosen sport it is necessary to have reached a high level of sporting performance. Thirteen per cent of the dyslexic students I have seen over the past nine years have represented their county at one or more sports. This figure of one in eight is much higher than would be expected in a typical UK university population. How then can this finding be explained?

There is an obvious answer and an alternative, more complicated explanation. The obvious reason is that sport represents an escape from the classroom for a number of dyslexic students. Therefore, these students will be highly motivated and devote more time to their chosen sports. This line of argument assumes that enthusiasm plus practice leads to excellence. However, I have seen too many people fail to be selected to represent their county even though they have the motivation and practise year after year. Another factor that is required for success is natural ability.

The next stage of the argument represents a speculative leap in thinking, for I'm now going to put forward the complex explanation. If one in eight dyslexic university students have excelled at a sport, this implies that there is a link, even if only a tenuous one, between being dyslexic and being good at sports. It is far from being a one-to-one association, but it occurs at above chance level. If this link exists, then excellent physical skills are precisely the kind of attributes that would have been advantageous in just about all societies and throughout the ages. In other words, such individuals would have had a head-start in most societies. In evolutionary terms, such individuals would have been favoured and this would cancel out the down side of being dyslexic. It is highly likely that individuals with excellent physical skills would have gained power and prestige in most societies, particularly if they were male.

We know from anthropology and history that men with power and prestige are likely to have more than one wife or female partner. Because of the inheritance factor this would result in the dyslexic gene clusters being widely distributed – amongst the most powerful and influential families of the time. Perhaps it is more than an interesting fact that I know of four royal families with dyslexic members.

Why a complication-free birth matters

There is one further twist to this line of speculation. Approximately one third of dyslexic students report a complication with their birth, such as a long and difficult labour, prematurity, or delivery by Caesarean section. However, whereas one in three dyslexic students report some form of birthing complication, as do two in three dyspraxic students, only one in seven male county-level dyslexic students, and one in eleven national-level male dyslexics, report such a complication. Somehow a complication-free birth seems to be linked with sporting ability.

This link can be considered in historical terms. Giving birth in the past was a very dangerous activity, partly because of poor diet, and partly because of lack of midwifery expertise. However, the wives of the powerful would have enjoyed a better diet than most – thus having a bigger gap in the pelvic bone for a baby's head to pass through, and would have had access to the best available midwifery assistance. Thus the incidence of birthing complications is likely to have been lower than for the wives of the general male population. This factor would therefore have played a part in ensuring the continuation of physical prowess – and the dyslexic gene pool.

I started off this chapter by stating that I would move from known factors to 'thinking outside the box' and I have advanced the proposition that dyslexia has a very long evolutionary history. Given that being dyslexic is associated with some negative factors, such as a weak working memory, there has to be a powerful reason why it has survived over millennia and across nations. The answer may be because it is, unexpectedly, associated in a tangential way with high levels of physical prowess and our evolutionary past. This is a speculative line of reasoning, some would say, 'way outside the box'. However, there is still much we don't know about dyslexia, and many questions remain to be answered.

The link between birth complications and poor motor coordination is much more obvious in the case of dyspraxics. In my experience about two in three dyspraxic students report a birth complication. However, it would be wrong to assume this does not mean that a good level of motor skill cannot be achieved. A survey of dyspraxic contemporary dance students (Quin et al., 2008) at a London dance conservatoire provides striking evidence of what can be achieved. By engaging in dance lessons over a long period of time training they had improved both muscular strength and posture and enhanced their own self-image. In addition, they had reached an elite level of dance. By choosing contemporary

dance over ballet there was less need to learn routines –
a dyspraxic weakness, whilst they had more opportunity
to improvise – a strength. The point to be made yet
again is that it is wise to avoid generalisations and to
focus instead on the individual.

Bibliography

Ellis, A.W. (1985) cited in Wolf, M. & O'Brien, B. (2001)
 'On issues of time, fluency, and intervention'. In Fawcett,
 A. (ed.) *Dyslexia: Theory and Good Practice*, Whurr
 Publishing, London (page 124).

Fisher, S.E. & DeFries, J.C. (2002) 'Developmental dyslexia:
 Genetic dissection of a complex cognitive trait', *Nature
 Reviews: Neuroscience*, 3, 767–780.

Grant, D. (2008) 'Sporting preferences and achievements of
 dyslexic and dyspraxic sports men and women: Lessons for
 London 2012?', *Dyslexia Review*, 20, 1, 31–37.

Quin, E., Wilkinson, J. & Hitchins, J. (January 2008) In-
 progress report of Phase I of the Trinity Laban TQEF
 funded project on *Dyspraxia in Music & Dance Students*,
 Trinity Laban Conservatoire of Music and Dance, London.

Stevenson, H.W., Stigler, J.W., Lucker, G.W. & Lee, S.
 (1982) 'Reading disabilities: The case of Chinese, Japanese,
 and English', *Child Development*, 53, 1164–1181.

Chapter 9

'Invisible' girls and women

There is a long-standing myth that many more males than females are dyslexic. It may also be a myth that many more males than females are dyspraxic. For a number of years I believed the figures for dyslexia to be true but, about nine years ago, I changed my mind about there being about three to four times more dyslexic males than females. There were two simple but powerful reasons for this change of opinion: I began meeting many more dyslexic women than men who had not previously been diagnosed and I came across recent research which challenged this myth about dyslexia. I am not the only one to have changed my mind. For example, the website of what was, in 2005, the UK government's Department for Education and Skills, drew attention to the idea that dyslexia may affect both sexes equally (www.dfes.gov.uk, 7 May 2005).

Over the past ten years I have carried out diagnostic assessments for more than 2,000 students. Very early on I was struck by two things. First, more women than men were referred to me for a diagnosis. Second, for every two men I saw and diagnosed as being dyslexic for the first time, I was seeing three women for whom this was their first diagnosis. More recently, when I looked at my data for dyspraxic students about five years ago, this type of discrepancy was even higher. To date I have seen more women than men who had not previously been diagnosed as being dyspraxic. Because my figures run so contrary to expectation – I anticipated seeing about three or four times as many dyspraxic men as women – it could mean only one thing. My figures suggested that girls who are dyslexic or dyspraxic are much more likely than boys to escape being diagnosed at school. Currently I am also starting to question whether the same is happening with ADHD. For example, Hallowell and Ratey (1994) suggest that three times as many males as females have ADHD. To date, I have seen almost equal numbers of men and women with ADHD.

In order to discover why so many girls missed out on being diagnosed while at school I listened to what students told me about their school experiences. Whereas some themes were common to both sexes, such as difficulties with concentration and being told 'you need to try harder', some comments occurred with much greater frequency for girls than boys. Many females described themselves as working much harder than other girls and taking care not to draw attention to themselves (see Illustration 9.1). Sharon spoke for many when she described how she tried to make herself invisible in class: 'I sat at the back of the class and hid behind the biggest girl in front of me.' She also tried to avoid catching the eye of the teacher. Farrah was typical of many who tried to avoid being asked questions in class: 'I tried to hide behind my books, I tried to sink into my desk.' Like many undiagnosed dyslexic and dyspraxic students Sharon and Farrah cut back on activities such as sports, music and social life in their mid-teen years to enable them to concentrate much more on their school work.

It has been my impression that a girl's sense of self-esteem is much more damaged than a boy's by having unexplained difficulties at school. This damage often begins in primary school when everyone else appears to understand what they have to do.

The feeling of being both different and inferior can then be compounded by being told off by the teacher for asking too many questions and being teased by other pupils for not being very bright. At secondary school the trend to a lowering of self-esteem is fed by being placed in low sets and increasing difficulties with homework. At this point avoidance strategies are adopted, such as asking to go to the toilet to avoid being asked to read aloud in class, or feigning illness to avoid going into school altogether. It is not surprising that some of the mature students I see found themselves pregnant when they were in their late teens. For some it is a new start towards rebuilding self-esteem.

Once again, as a rough generalisation, boys appear to adopt a different set of strategies in response to difficulties with academic work. When John described how he became 'the joker' in his year, he spoke for a number of boys. It was his way of distracting the other boys' attention from his real academic difficulties. In a number of cases male students have described how they became disruptive in class. Probably the extreme case

Illustration 9.1

was Tony. He described how he became so frustrated at being told off by his maths teacher for not doing his homework that he hit the teacher. Following his suspension from school he was assessed and found to be severely dyslexic. His local education authority then arranged for him to go to a boarding school that specialised in teaching dyslexic pupils. Tony said this was 'the best thing that happened to me'. Other boys find that sporting activities provide them with an outlet that gives them status at school, an outlet that is less attractive to many girls.

I am not the first to suggest that the different ways in which boys and girls respond to difficulties result in boys being noticed while girls fade into the background. In 1999, Wagner and Garon described the outcome of a longitudinal survey that followed a group of American schoolchildren from kindergarten to graduation. Over this period of time children with reading difficulties were identified in two different ways. When teacher reports were used as the basis, about three times as many boys were identified as having reading difficulties as girls. However, when a research approach was applied and all children were assessed, the numbers of boys and girls with reading problems were almost equal. The study concluded that 'the difference in the prevalence of reading disability between boys and girls appears to be an artefact of referral bias. Boys tend to be more disruptive than girls and consequently are more likely to be referred' (page 89).

The observation that a research approach to the identification of reading difficulties results in finding almost as many girls as boys have reading problems is matched by an almost identical finding from a major survey that used a research approach across three countries – the USA, Korea and Japan. (This work of Stevenson et al., 1982, is also referred to in Chapter 6.) Explanation of gender differences based on the impact of male hormones on the developing brain, or the influence of the male X chromosome, (e.g. Jones, 2002) would appear to be – at the least – open to serious questioning.

Trying to determine gender differences on the basis of counting how many males and how many females have been referred for assessment has always been known to be a potential source of error. That is why I have been very cautious about my own data. However, because UK colleges and universities have become much more pro-active and positive about providing support for students with a range of specific learning difficulties, undiagnosed students have – often for the first time – had an opportunity to disclose their genuine difficulties, difficulties that they have often hidden from many people. The invisible are slowly becoming visible. For example, Kerry was first diagnosed as having dyspraxia and ADHD only when she was an undergraduate, in spite of the many occasions she fell off her chair at school through being fidgety. Her illustration of herself in school captures her sense of being 'left out and different' (see Illustration 9.2).

There is still a long way to go and, if dyslexia is a hidden learning difficulty, dyspraxia and ADHD are even more hidden. It is also my experience that dyslexia

Illustration 9.2

is even more invisible in children with English as an additional language. While it is easy to attribute a child's difficulties with learning to read and spell in English as being due to his or her family using Polish, or Chinese, or Urdu at home, close questioning often reveals, in the case of dyslexia, a cluster of typical behaviours and experiences, such as a tendency to be forgetful, or slow at writing. Dyslexia, dyspraxia and ADHD do not respect gender or nationality. Cultural expectations, whether of gender or ethnicity, can hinder rather than facilitate the search for the true situation.

While it is very important to be aware of the power of gender-based beliefs, it would be misleading to leave the impression that this is the sole reason why more girls than boys are not diagnosed as being dyslexic. There is another factor at work. Even at birth girls are biologically advanced compared with boys and this difference widens over the years. By the time of puberty – a word that literally means to become hairy – this biological difference is one of more than twelve months. However, the publishers of tests do not take account of this difference. Instead of calculating an average score for girls, and another average score for boys, they calculate an average without taking sex into account. Consequently, the average girl will perform better on a test than an average boy. This in turn means that more boys will score below average, and there will be more boys in the lowest scoring groups. Consequently, if a teacher relies just on class tests, more boys will appear to be at risk than girls.

Biology, combined with gender-related cultural expectations, masks the genuine difficulties that dyslexic girls experience at school. I suspect that the same factors are at work for girls with dyspraxia and ADHD as well.

Bibliography

Hallowell, E.M. & Ratey, J.J. (1995) *Driven to Distraction: Recognising and Coping with Attention Deficit Disorder from Childhood through Adulthood*, Touchstone, New York.
Jones, S. (2002) *Y: The Descent of Men*, Little, Brown, London.
Stevenson, H.W., Stigler, J.W., Lucker, G.W. & Lee, S. (1982) 'Reading disabilities: The case of Chinese, Japanese, and English', *Child Development*, 53, 1164–1181.
Wagner, R.K. & Garon, T. (1999) 'Learning disabilities in perspective'. In Sternberg, R.J. & Spear-Swerling, L. (eds) *Perspectives on Learning Disabilities: Biological, Cognitive, Contextual*, Westview Press, Oxford.

Chapter 10

Sleep

Which statement best describes you?

1 When I go to bed and close my eyes I usually fall asleep quickly.
2 When I go to bed and close my eyes I have difficulty getting to sleep because my mind buzzes with thoughts.

In general, only about one in four university students report frequent difficulties with getting to sleep. However, when dyslexic students are asked whether they fall asleep quickly, about 60 to 65 per cent report having problems (Grant, 2004). That is, about two to three times as many dyslexic students report frequent difficulties with getting to sleep as non-dyslexic students.

When I asked Hannah to draw an illustration that captured this feature of dyslexic life she immediately knew what I was talking about. She is dyslexic herself and has trouble getting to sleep. As you can see in her illustration (Illustration 10.1), she also keeps a notebook by her bedside – something that at least one in six

Illustration 10.1

dyslexic students do. They do this because they know that if they don't jot down an important idea as soon as it occurs to them they are likely to forget it by the following morning.

Difficulty with getting to sleep has previously been reported as being characteristic of dyspraxics (e.g. Portwood, 2000) and ADHD (e.g. Brown, 2005) but not, as far as I know, of dyslexics. Why, then, has this been overlooked? It probably stems from the very definition of dyslexia. Most definitions of dyslexia are very narrow as they concentrate on either reading and writing or phonological processing. They do not concern themselves with the everyday experiences of being dyslexic. The consequence of this narrow definition is a narrow approach to research. Virtually all research on dyslexia focuses on language and literacy, while the more general aspects of being dyslexic are ignored. However, the definition of dyspraxia is much broader. Consequently most books about dyspraxia take a much more holistic approach and it is easier to form a more rounded picture of the individual.

In order to gain an understanding of what it is really like to be dyslexic, it is necessary to spend time exploring wider aspects of everyday life. Ever since listening to a dyslexic student talk about her difficulties with getting to sleep some years ago I have made a point of asking all the dyslexic students I see about their experience of getting to sleep. The common history of a difficulty with falling asleep emerged almost immediately. When asked what thoughts and ideas occurred during the period of time before drifting off to sleep, a majority described how they use the time to sort through the day's events and plan for the following day.

They often point out that ideas, sometimes good or important ones, just 'pop' into their minds. They also frequently say that because they know they have difficulties with remembering they take steps to write these ideas down, even though they are in bed, because they know that otherwise they would have forgotten the idea by the time they wake up the following morning. Very often they mention they feel more relaxed having noted an idea down. Not everyone keeps a notepad by the side of their bed. Some students use their mobile phones as organisers, and one student described how helpful she found it to have a whiteboard at her bedside. As she had previously written ideas down on scraps of paper, which she then lost, she knew she could not lose the whiteboard.

The second most common theme that students report is creative thinking. However, in comparison with the numbers who mention 'sorting through the day's events and planning for tomorrow', thinking creatively is much less prevalent. Creative thinking is also, for some students, interlinked with thinking through the events of the day if they have spent the day working hard on an assignment.

For some students, getting to sleep can take so long and is so disruptive that they have experimented with different strategies to help them fall asleep. A common technique is to play a CD 'I've heard a 1,000 times before' to help blot out ideas. Other strategies include watching a film on television, using meditation, drinking camomile tea, and having a warm bath. Surprising as it may seem – to a non-dyslexic – reading rapidly induces sleepiness in some dyslexics. Therefore, some students deliberately start reading to help them fall asleep. There does not appear to be a magic technique that will work for everyone. What works for some people, such as playing a CD, keeps others awake.

Why is it that so many dyslexics, dyspraxics and individuals with ADHD find it difficult to get to sleep? The fact that it occurs for all groups provides a clue, for common to them all is a weak working memory. The night-time thinking period is frequently taken up with sorting through the day's events and planning for the following day: 'What did he/she mean when they said that?', 'Have I got time to do that tomorrow?', 'I must not forget to do that.' Ideas and thoughts 'pop' into consciousness at random, sometimes only for a fleeting moment. A short poem that Sue composed for me captures this experience perfectly.

> As I lie awake in bed
> Poems come floating through my head.
> I try to grasp them, grab them, catch them,
> But somehow I just can't nab them.

If you listen to a dyslexic, dyspraxic or individual with ADHD describing their thought patterns when they are trying to get to sleep, at times it sounds very much as if their mind is trying to restore order to chaos. To help understand what is going on it is helpful to consider the role of working memory. Working memory is a mental survival process. It enables us to bring into consciousness memories of past events as well as thoughts about the future. It enables us to be aware of what we have done as well as what we could do. It is vital to survival. When someone has an active life but a working memory deficit, working memory will be overworked throughout the daytime. As a consequence, it is as if many thoughts don't get processed and there is a backlog of unfinished work by the end of the day. At bedtime there is a sudden drop in external stimulation. It's much quieter and it's dark. Because of this drop in external stimulation working memory can begin to function more effectively and this enables unfinished business from the day to be resolved. It is a form of mental clearing up.

Although this analogy has a simplicity to it that appears to capture what is going on, it is unlikely to be the whole story. Another factor to consider is stress. A weak working memory and a slow speed of visual processing will impede the rate of learning. This immediately places those students with dyslexia, dyspraxia or ADHD at a disadvantage when they are required to work and learn at the same pace as other students. Stress will give rise to anxiety which, in turn, will affect the ease with which someone can fall asleep. Stress should not be discounted as an important factor. However, descriptions by students with dyslexia, dyspraxia or ADHD of what they think about suggest that thoughts about sorting through the day's events and planning for the following day are much more frequent than the type of thoughts that would be typical of someone under a high degree of stress.

It is important to remember that not all people with dyslexia, dyspraxia or ADHD have difficulties with getting to sleep, and about 25 per cent of the general undergraduate population have trouble getting to sleep. Also, a small minority of those with dyslexia, dyspraxia or ADHD do not consider that taking an hour or more to fall asleep is a 'difficulty'. Typically, they have always spent considerable time thinking before falling asleep, and believe this must be the case for everyone else as well. Nevertheless, the frequency with which they report difficulties with getting to sleep reveals that this is an important but overlooked feature. A number of dyslexic, dyspraxic and ADHD students experience this difficulty throughout their life and a few find it quite disruptive. A surprising number report staying up late – and often say they are the last one in their student flat or house to go to bed because they know that getting to sleep will be such a long process. Consequently, getting up then becomes a problem.

When I first presented my survey revealing dyslexics' difficulties with getting to sleep, a tutor, who was herself dyslexic, carried out a brief survey of her dyslexic colleagues. She was amazed to discover that, like herself, they all said they had problems getting to sleep, and they all kept a notebook by their bedside. Not one of them had appreciated that this was a typical dyslexic characteristic. At the end of telling me about her mini-survey, the tutor asked a very pertinent question: 'How much more is there to discover about the experience of being dyslexic?'

Bibliography

Brown, T.E. (2005) *Attention Deficit Disorder: The Unfocused Mind in Children and Adults*, Yale University Press, Cambridge, MA.

Grant, D. (2004) 'From myths to realities: Lessons to be drawn about dyslexia from over 900 student assessments', paper presented at the 6th BDA International Conference at Warwick, March.

Portwood, M. (2000) *Understanding Developmental Dyspraxia*, David Fulton Publishers, London.

Chapter 11

Neurodiversity and concluding remarks

There are two consistent themes running throughout this book: individuality and commonality. These are not contradictory, but rather complementary aspects of understanding how variations in fundamental cognitive processes colour and shape the everyday behaviours and experiences of individuals with specific learning differences. Because the cognitive profile of strengths and weaknesses varies from one person to another, diagnostic categories are imperfect, in that they imply uniformity and clear-cut boundaries. The reality is very different. It is these elements of individuality and blurring of boundaries that have led a number of individuals with specific learning differences to prefer the description of being neurodiverse.

The term 'neurodiversity' is a recent one that appears to have first been used in 1998 by Singer as a positive way of describing individuals who are autistic. Within a short period of time it began to be adopted as a positive way of stating that the brains of individuals with specific learning differences (including dyslexia, dyspraxia and ADHD) are wired differently from those of neurotypicals (NTs). The adoption of this term can be seen as a commitment to a social model of disability, for when it is used it means: 'Yes, I am different, but I want to be accepted for who I am, not what society would like me to be.' It also implies that the neurotypical society should implement changes to accommodate and respect specific learning differences rather than to seek cures for them. The social model of disability is a rejection of the medical model, with its reliance on terms such as 'dysfunction', 'disorder', 'symptoms' and 'co-morbidity'.

The use of the phrase 'specific learning difference' instead of 'specific learning difficulty' has been adopted specifically to reflect the fact that there are many different ways of learning. In historical terms, the relative newness of having to learn and work mainly through reading and writing rather than through listening, seeing and doing has resulted in significant numbers of individuals being disadvantaged. In order to know how to improve the everyday experiences of the neurodiverse in a world designed for the neurotypical, it is first necessary to understand the cognitive and sensory worlds of the neurodiverse. Those worlds, explored in this book, are undoubtedly complex, complicated and very varied.

Regrettably there is a long way to go before the social model of disability becomes widely accepted and implemented. Even working within the current model of diagnosis and dysfunction many neurodiverse individuals still experience many years of negativity and low self-esteem. When Laura told me, 'I have learnt to live with who I am', she spoke for many undiagnosed dyslexics, dyspraxics and individuals with ADHD. Throughout her life she had known she did some things differently from many other people, and found some things difficult that others found easy, but she had never known why. At the end of her assessment, and following a discussion of how her profile of strengths and weaknesses was reflected in her personal history, it was as if an enormous burden had been lifted from her. She was still the same person, but now, at long last, she had an explanation.

My motivation to write this book came from meeting many people like Laura. Because being dyslexic, dyspraxic or an individual with ADHD shapes, colours and influences so many aspects of everyday life, it is appropriate to describe being dyslexic or dyspraxic or having ADHD as really being a lifestyle. Consequently this book covers a number of different aspects of everyday life and provides explanations for them.

For example, difficulties with memory are frequently observed in a range of specific learning differences and affect a wide range of experiences, such as remembering where you have just placed an item, taking in information in a briefing, and remembering the names of people you have just met. A weak working memory also creates difficulties with determining the order of ideas in an essay or report, and with sentence structure. More surprisingly, problems with remembering may also help explain why so many dyslexics and dyspraxics have trouble getting to sleep. From the time of waking up to the time of falling asleep, dyslexia, dyspraxia and ADHD influence how many aspects of daily life are experienced.

It is not therefore unexpected that this shapes the kind of careers dyslexics, dyspraxics and individuals with

ADHD select for themselves. The chapter on being creative develops a new way of thinking about why dyslexia and creativity are often linked together. Being creative requires long spells of hard work. Dyslexics – and dyspraxics – are so used to having to work harder than others that it is not surprising that this degree of commitment successfully spills over into the workplace. In providing explanations it has, at times, been necessary to dispel myths about dyslexia and dyspraxia. For example, if we believe that dyslexia and dyspraxia are predominantly associated with being male, then dyslexic and dyspraxic girls and women are likely to be overlooked. I have presented evidence that reveals that dyslexia and dyspraxia are more common in females than many have believed, and have sought to explain why this gender bias has occurred. I have a suspicion this gender bias extends to ADHD as well.

The relationship between mental imagery and specific learning differences has also been explored. The oft stated belief that dyslexics are visual thinkers finds some support in this exploration. However, it is quite clear it is not the case that all dyslexics are visual thinkers. Intriguingly the variation in mental imagery is even more extreme in individuals with ADHD and it is suggested that the high incidence of synaesthesia in individuals with ADHD may be a reflection of the same underlying neurological mechanism of disinhibition.

More controversially, ideas concerning the universal nature of dyslexia and its evolutionary history have been explored. It is proposed that being dyslexic is an experience that, many millennia ago, was a survival advantage, and this factor may account for why dyslexia and sporting prowess are linked.

Of all the ideas explored in this book, perhaps the two most important are that it is much more helpful to recognise the different forms that dyslexia, dyspraxia and ADHD take, and to realise that they are more similar than dissimilar. This then enables us to recognise people's individuality and arrive at explanations that make sense. Through understanding comes liberation and empowerment. Laura spoke for so many when, at the conclusion of her diagnostic assessment, she said: 'I can now put my demons behind me and plan for a new future.'

Bibliography

Singer, J. (1998) 'Odd people in: The birth of community amongst people on the autistic spectrum: a personal exploration of a new social movement based on neurological diversity'. Honours Dissertation, University of Technology, Sydney (available via www.neurodiversity. com.au/lightdark.htm).

Further reading and information

Pollak, D. (2009) Neurodiversity in Higher Education: Positive Responses to Specific Learning Differences, Wiley-Blackwell, West Sussex.
DANDA (Developmental Adult Neuro-Diversity Association) www.DANDA.org.uk.

Appendix

Suppliers of assistive software

There is a wide range of assistive software now available. There are frequent updates of current software. New products are introduced on a fairly regular basis. Most assistive software is not available from high-street shops. There are several major web-based suppliers in the UK. iansyst and Microlink PC have over a decade's experience in supplying assistive hardware and software to higher education students with specific learning difficulties. They can also provide training.

iansyst Ltd: www.iansyst.co.uk
Inclusive Technology: www.inclusive.co.uk
Microlink PC: www.microlinkpc.co.uk